❧❦ Advance Praise

"Lots of 'experts' write books about loss. Doctors, PhD's, pastors, therapists. But nobody can write a real book about loss better than someone who has lived it. Myra McElhaney's memoir about losing the love of her life takes us through all the stages: from her beautiful life before diagnosis, her husband's heartbreaking death, Myra's unimaginable grief, and into her beautiful new life. She holds nothing back. We see it all. Raw and honest and yes, even funny. If you are suffering loss, I urge you to let Myra's story help you navigate the waters of this very difficult storm. She is bright, shining, living proof that joy does indeed wait on the other side."

Kimberley Kennedy, TV journalist and author, *Left at the Altar*

"Myra's warm, wise, welcoming voice makes you feel like you're sitting next to her sharing a cup of tea, coffee, or perhaps a livelier libation. She shows how a sassy outlook and a sense of humor can be a saving grace when dealing with loss, grief, and sorrow. You'll be ready to enjoy life again—and see it as the blessing it is—as a result of her inspiring insights and stories. Read them and reap."

Sam Horn, Author of *Tongue Fu!* and *Got Your Attention?*

"In the many years that I have known Myra, I have always been one of her biggest admirers, watching as she crawled her way out of a young life that wasn't much of anything special and ran toward a fully robust, adventurous life. She is a determined fighter but no more so than when, devastated, she had to pull insights and self-awareness from her reserves of resilience to survive the profound loss of the love of her life. Even while Myra voiced heart-numbing anguish and anger with God, you see glimpses of the sassiness and humor that has always defined my friend. And now with authentic storytelling swerve, you feel like you're riding along with Myra as she determinedly reinvents life and finds joy again."

Ronda Rich, Bestselling Author and Syndicated Columnist

"Although there's nothing funny about losing the love of your life, you'll laugh through the tears as Myra shares her personal stories of moving forward after her husband's passing. The warmth and brutal honesty she shares in this compelling memoir of sorrow and resilience will encourage and inspire anyone who has lost someone they love."

Connie Glaser, Bestselling Author and Syndicated Columnist

"Myra McElhaney's *Building a Life You Love After Losing the Love of Your Life* is a book about resilience and grit. When her husband was diagnosed with a deadly tumor, McElhaney faced a terrible test of her courage. The book tells the story of how she negotiated with herself to care for him, to grieve in a way that worked for her, to honor his memory, and to eventually move forward. Full of candor and practical advice, it offers lessons that can be applied by not only those who are bereaved but by anyone struggling with a profound loss."

Carol Frohlinger, President, Negotiating Women, Inc.

"A well-told story of loss and return to life. Through her own tears and laughter, you will find this story as courageous and hopeful, even practical, as it is heartbreaking. Thank you, Myra for this gift of strength and resilience."

Cynthia Good, Founder & CEO, LittlePinkBook.com

"Myra's confidence and courage is apparent as she shares her story of profound loss. Even in the depths of sorrow her trademark humor peeks through as she talks of pajama days and grief therapy with Ben & Jerry. I know that widows and widowers will find wisdom in her insights and her anecdotes will encourage them to be bold in finding strength after loss."

Becky Blalock, Author, *DARE: Straight Talk on Confidence, Courage, and Career for Women in Charge*

"Though writer Myra McElhaney didn't choose the journey of widowhood, she has ended up giving us a treasure. This beautifully written story of love, loss, and transition offers hope to all of us that, after a devastating loss, we can move forward with grace."

Jennifer B. Kahnweiler, Ph.D. Author of *The Genius of Opposites, Quiet Influence,* and *The Introverted Leader*

"Myra McElhaney shares a deeply personal account of her journey with unflinching and raw honesty in a way that is both practical and inspirational. Anyone who has experienced the loss of a great love will recognize the kaleidoscope of emotions and struggles universal for the mourning that Ms. McElhaney shares in her funny and, at times, heartbreaking book. A sort of 'guide' for the grieving, I will encourage my clients to read this book because of the clear message that there is abundant hope for life and love after loss."

Meg McLeroy, Marriage and Family Therapist

"Myra captivates from the first word. Her wry sense of humor will have you smiling through the tears at every turn and even laughing aloud at the ridiculousness that life can deliver. She paints a picture of how to let go of loss and find yourself again— even when you'd rather stay lost in grief. This book is like having a friend who's been where you are, knows just what to say to pull you through the darkest bits, and is there to celebrate when you start to see the light again. I honestly couldn't put it down and have shared it with friends, clients, and total strangers, yes it is that good!"

Melissa Galt, Author, *Celebrate Your Life* and *Move It Forward: 31 Days to a More Prosperous You in Business and Life*

"Kudos to Myra for candidly sharing the messiness and blessings of life after death. I wish I had this to read when I lost my husband in 1997. With Myra's purpose of enjoying life and doing good, she couldn't help but write such an inspiring and empowering book."

Tricia Molloy, Author, *Working with Wisdom*

"Anyone who has lost a life partner understands just how unbearable it is. For those of us in this unfortunate club, Myra has written a real, yet encouraging tale of her effort to make a path to the sort of life her husband would have wished for her. Her honesty about each day's struggle will comfort and help those of you who worry about someone like us who is trying to survive one of life's greatest unfairnesses."

Nate Bennett, Author, *Shannon's Gift: A Story of Love, Loss, and Recovery*

"My mother lost the love of her life and I lost the pillar of my life when my Dad died. Myra perfectly captures the laundry-like cycle of emotions—including laughter—that you go through when you are a caregiver to someone you love. Then, she realistically shows us how we can create something new and wonderful with the washed-out pieces remaining after they are gone."

Bonnie B. Daneker, author of *The Compassionate Caregiver Series*®

"This is a very good book. It will help many people who go through the loss of a love or any big turning point in a life lived to the fullest. Myra McElhaney tells her story with engaging style and amazing grace. I hope every one of my friends and the entire "Possible Woman" community reads Myra's book, just for the joy of a good story about a very talented and gifted woman. Her journey is one of hope and faith as she faces what is real and grows through the pain of loss. Her message gives good insight into a life well lived."

Marjorie R. Barlow, Ph.D., Author, *The Possible Woman Steps Up: Women's Leadership in the 21st Century*

"A delightful gift from the heart. Go elsewhere if you are looking for the reason for or the lessons to be learned from loss. Instead read these words that simply and eloquently describe the grief of losing a partner. From the gut wrenching sense of loss to the anger against well-wishers to the bittersweet memories, you will recognize the shared journey of grief. As a 'widow lady' myself, I love the empathy, the irreverence and the courage of this story."

Sandra Hofmann, Community Gadfly, Board Director, Choosing to live and love every day!

"Myra takes us on her unintentional hero's journey of transformation filled with genuine warmth, unwavering hope and solidly grounded insight. We experience Myra's gritty southern resilience as she struggles with the ubiquitous challenges of life—resolving feelings of despair, understanding God's grace, and searching for life's meaning. Myra's writing juxtaposes old soul wisdom with red convertible sparkle to remind us that no matter the challenge we face, we can build a life that we love."

Susan Reece, Ph.D., HR Executive

"This book is bold! It's thought-provoking and often laughter-inducing as Myra opens her heart and soul, giving readers a personal and profound glimpse of how she managed to live again after losing the love of her life. She's vulnerable, raw, spiritual, humorous, and irreverently reverent. Get ready to mourn, cry, laugh, and even gasp as Myra finds joy again. Most of all, find inspiration for coping when you don't have any cope left."

Dr. Shirley Garrett, Author, *A Tap Water Girl in a Bottled Water World*

"Myra's effort validates practically every feeling I experienced after my wife's death, also from cancer. It all seemed so familiar. I only wish that I had this book as a reference in those dark times."

Bill Asbell, Attorney, Asbell Rhoads LLP

"Myra McElhaney's memoir is a poignant and lively guidebook for navigating through one of the most difficult chapters in life: the loss of a spouse. Her journey from despair to hope is told with wisdom, sass, and wit."

Bobbi Kornblit, author of *Shelter from the Texas Heat: a novel*

"There's nothing funny about losing the love of your life but Myra beautifully blends humor and heartbreak as she lets us peek in to her pain and process of choosing to move forward in her life. Grab your hanky and hang on as this talented insightful writer takes you to places you will laugh through your tears. Those crazy widow days she shares will make you wonder how she got though. Brilliantly written, this book will not only changes lives, I believe it will save some by giving them hope in how to rebuild a life they can love."

June Cline, CSP, Humorist Bestselling author, and radio host

"Myra's beautifully written, poignant book is full of life changing advice on how to carry on in the face of loss. Whether you have lost the love of your life, your job, or your confidence, you will be comforted and inspired."

Nadia Bilchik, CNN Editorial Producer

Building a Life You Love

AFTER

Losing the Love of Your Life

MYRA McELHANEY

You Can find
Joy again!
myra

ISBN: 978-0-9971547-0-2

Library of Congress Control Number: 2015920981

Cover and interior layout design by: Vanessa Lowry
Editing by: Nanette Littlestone
Convertible photo on cover and author photos by: Lorikay Stone
Road photo on cover: © Helenrempel | Dreamstime.com
Storm photo on cover: © Baloncici | Dreamstime.com

This book may be purchased in bulk for educational, business, fundraising or sales promotional use. For information please contact:
Myra McElhaney, www.MyraMcElhaney.com

In loving memory of Phil McElhaney,
the love of my life.

Death leaves a heartache no one can heal; love leaves a memory no one can steal.

From an Irish headstone

Table of Contents

Sometimes what looks like
courage is just fear pointed
in the right direction.

Myra McElhaney

Introduction

If you're reading this book you've probably lost your love, too. I'm sorry for your loss and sad that you've joined this club where no one wants to be a member. Hang in there. It's been years for me now and I can tell you that it does get easier. Sometimes it feels like one step forward and two steps back, or is it the other way around? Anyway, you can survive. With determination you can even thrive. I believe that through sharing our stories—the good, the bad, and the ugly—we can encourage each other and find comfort in knowing others have made it through grief to find joy again.

In 2007 my husband Phil and I celebrated our fiftieth birthdays with a trip to China. He was top salesman in the company where he worked in the telecommunications industry, right on track for his plan of retiring early, and wanted to travel the world. I'd spent a couple years writing and researching a book for women. After collecting a stack of rejection letters I finally found an agent in New York who'd agreed to work with me. She was already discussing my book with publishers. We'd just moved into our dream home where we had plenty of room to entertain family and friends. It was the happiest time of our lives.

Phil had been having some "weird" headaches where everything went white. I thought maybe it was migraines with an aura. He seemed concerned but hadn't yet made an appointment with his doctor to have it checked out.

On Friday, December 7th I was in the shower when Phil came home. Even without seeing him I knew something was wrong. He came into the bathroom, mumbled something, and went back out. The absence of his usual, cheerful "Hello!" and playful greeting seemed odd.

Straight from the shower I went to the living room to see him, my wet hair wrapped in a towel. The sight of him sitting on the sofa staring at the fireplace with a strained, confused look on his face instead of the usual smile and twinkling eyes bothered me. When I asked what was wrong he said, "Something is but I don't know what."

His concerned look and tone of voice was chilling.

I asked if he had a headache. He said, "Yes."

"Does your chest hurt?" I asked.

"Yes."

"Your stomach?"

"Yes."

"I'm calling Dr. Herron."

Phil shook his head slowly indicating that he didn't know who I was referring to.

"Herron, Herring, what's his name?" I said, realizing I may have gotten the name wrong as I often do. He shook his head again. The alarmed look in his eyes stopped me cold. Phil was a detail oriented engineer. He never forgot names, dates, or facts. Now he didn't know the name of the doctor he'd been seeing for over twenty years. I asked more questions.

"Who am I?"

"My wife." Thank God he knew that!

"Where do you work?"

He looked around as if searching for a clue. "Here?" he questioned.

"Yes, you work from home but what's the name of the company?" He shook his head again.

"I'm taking you to the emergency room," I said calmly, masking the fear I felt. He said that he didn't know if that was a good idea but he didn't protest much as I hurriedly dressed and combed through my wet hair.

Along the way I asked other questions. He didn't know the name of the CEO of his company with whom he'd just spent a week traveling. He did know his mother's name and his brother's, so that was somehow encouraging. He also shared with me that he'd gotten a couple phone calls as he drove home from his business trip. He couldn't understand the words the callers were saying so he told them he'd have to call them back.

The ER waiting room was miraculously empty. I ran in the door calling out that I needed help because my husband couldn't remember where he worked and they got us into the triage area rather quickly. By the time we'd made the short five-minute drive to the hospital and he got in to see a doctor the episode had passed and his memory was fully recovered.

"This is some sort of brain seizure," the doctor said, asking if he'd had anything like it in the past. To my surprise, Phil admitted that he had. A couple weeks earlier he couldn't understand the words when he was trying to read the paper.

"We'll run some tests, rule out some of the bigger issues, and then you can see your regular doctor to work on finding the cause of these seizures," the doctor said, explaining that the cause is sometimes hard to pinpoint.

We were moved to an exam room and Phil was taken for tests while I made calls to cancel the dinner party we had planned for later that evening. I also called the two co-workers who had phoned during his drive home and both reported that they had not suspected anything wrong. He seemed distracted and said he'd call them back. They both chalked it up to him having another call coming in.

He was driving and talking on the phone while having a brain seizure. Scary thought.

If you've ever been to the emergency room, you know it takes a long time to be cleared to leave. Phil and I were both hungry so we ordered Chinese food from across the street and ate in the exam room while waiting for the doctor to come in and release him. As the doctor walked in the door we both reached for our jackets and began putting them on as he spoke.

"We've completed the tests," he began innocently enough. "We found a mass on your brain." Phil and I both stared at him silently as we tried to comprehend what he'd just said.

"I'm not a brain surgeon but if it's what I think it is, you'll have twelve to eighteen months to live." Stunned, we kept staring as he continued. I was waiting for the "here's how we fix it" part. That never came. He told us that the brain surgeon on-call was on his way to the hospital and they'd like to admit Phil to do a biopsy and make sure what they were dealing with.

"I'm going home," Phil said calmly, reaching for his keys.

"Is that okay with you?" the doctor asked, turning toward me.

If he was looking to me to intervene that must be critical, right? I began asking questions. The doctor explained that since it was the weekend and Phil was being admitted via the emergency room, the biopsy would be done right away. If we went home and came back it would have to be scheduled, like a non-emergency, and we would waste valuable days in getting the exact diagnosis. He assured us that once the biopsy was done we would be able to get other opinions and look outside their hospital to make treatment decisions. Phil agreed to be admitted and was sent to Neuro-ICU.

After weeks of waiting for the results it was confirmed that he had a Glioblastoma Multiforme (GBM), Stage IV. The deadliest, most aggressive malignant brain tumor known to man.

Our lives had changed instantly in that emergency room visit.

From work, traveling, entertaining, and planning for retirement we went to having our lives revolve around doctors, hospitals, tests, surgery, and treatments. We chose to focus on the possibilities, not the prognosis, determined to enjoy every day as best we could. We traveled and entertained as much as his treatment schedule and energy would allow. Our family and friends surrounded us with amazing support, love, and understanding. We went to the Preston Robert Tish Brain Tumor Center at Duke University where the rock star of brain surgeons removed the tumor. In only five short months it was back with a vengeance.

Phil died, June 4, 2009 at the age of 51. Eighteen months after being diagnosed.

This is where my story starts. We had a joyful life together and were looking forward to early retirement. I never thought "till death do us part" would come so soon. During the eighteen months between his diagnosis and death I didn't give a thought to what would happen "after." That would have required me to acknowledge that he could actually die. I couldn't do that.

After the funeral I wallowed in sorrow and self-pity for a while then realized that it apparently takes a long, long time to eat and drink yourself to death. I didn't want to live without him but since I was still here I might as well get up and get on with life.

You probably know what I mean.

I believe that having tragedy in your life doesn't mean your life has to be a tragedy. I claimed that belief early on, although on some days it was more of an aspiration than an affirmation. Let's just say I grew into it. I figure that if I'm going to choose a genre for my life I'll pick "romantic comedy." I've had romance and believe it's possible again. I've had tragedy. As for comedy, they say that's just tragedy plus time. I can look back and laugh now at many things that didn't seem so funny while I was living them. Maybe they're right.

I love to give advice and wish that I had some magic formula for fast-forwarding through grief. Or even twenty tips to make it easier. I don't. All I can do is share my story. I hope that through reading mine you'll find hope, encouragement, and comfort for living your own.

• • •

Just because there has
been tragedy in your life
doesn't mean your life
has to be a tragedy.

Myra McElhaney

CHAPTER 1

In Bed with Jose Cuervo

"I'm going to bed with a bottle of Jose Cuervo. If I'm not out in two weeks come get me."

I said that to my sister Cynthia the day after my husband's burial. She and some friends had been hovering over me every minute since Phil died. Now they didn't want to leave me alone in our big house consumed with grief.

Maybe they thought that without someone to keep an eye on me I'd melt into a puddle of snot and tears. Like the wicked witch in the Wizard of Oz when Dorothy doused her with water. Just melt into the floor, dissolved in grief, leaving only a black suit and sensible pumps in the spot where I stood.

It had been a long few days. Since the day Phil died from a brain tumor, I'd been surrounded with family and friends. There had been people coming and going, staying in our house day and night. Not to mention the eighteen months of caregiving that had passed since his diagnosis. Even before Phil was sick it wasn't uncommon for us to have guests in all four guest bedrooms from time to time. Many of our friends were so familiar with our house that they, plus my sister Cynthia had been pretty much running it the last few weeks.

Since the Day of Death someone had told me what time to be dressed and ready, who was driving me where, and even when to eat. Sometimes I was guided to a table, gently pushed into a chair, a plate of food placed in front of me and someone would say, "It's time for you to eat."

Now I wanted them to all go away. I was exhausted—physically, mentally and emotionally. I needed to see if I could stand on my own two feet. But first I needed sleep. I wanted to sleep for at least a week. I needed to close my eyes and shut out everything and everyone. At least in my dreams I wasn't missing Phil.

I just wanted to stay in bed. I wouldn't be sleeping with "one eye open," so to speak, in case Phil needed me during the night. I'd give anything in the world to have my husband back but he was gone. It was time to give in to my own exhaustion and get a good night's sleep. No appointments, no treatments, no medicine doses to give, no calls to or from doctors or funeral homes. Just sleep. No thinking. No talking. No listening. No bathing.

The next morning I awoke with no voice. (Didn't I say no talking?) Headache, congestion, sore throat, and no voice.

Some flu-virus-infection thing had taken advantage of my weakened state and grabbed hold. Before heading home, Cynthia called a doctor-friend who called in a prescription for a Z-Pack and said if I wasn't better after taking the 3-day dose of Azithromycin antibiotic to come in for an examination. She prescribed fluids and bed rest, exactly what I needed. Cynthia picked up the medicine from the pharmacy, stocked the refrigerator with appropriate liquids, put tissues on the nightstand for easy reach, and tearfully headed to her own home. She couldn't stop my pain or fix it for me but she did her best to make sure I was okay.

With all the friends and family gone and the house quiet, I gave in to my sorrow and exhaustion. The medication helped me to sleep and helped my weakened body to mend.

It isn't uncommon for people who have lost a loved one to become sick immediately after. The stress of illness and death takes a toll on the immune system and drains the body of energy. When you're taking care of someone who is critically ill, you often shut out the needs of your own body for things like sleep, relaxation, and nutrition. Some folks don't eat. For others, emotional eating takes over. Once the crisis has passed the body needs what it needs. Usually it demands rest. Getting sick is one way the body smacks you upside the head with the need for rest.

So I went to bed with a Z-pack instead of Jose Cuervo. And before the invitations to AA meetings start coming in, my "going to bed with Jose Cuervo" statement was just my irreverent sense of humor coming out. A figure of speech. I wanted to numb the pain but getting soused wasn't the plan. Sleep was. I was surprised later to realize that several friends thought I was really drinking tequila in my bedroom. Nope. In the kitchen though. And the living room. And a pub or two. Or three. And a few good Mexican restaurants.

The Depths of Despair

"Why does the sun go on shining?" The lyrics of an old song kept playing in my head. "The End of The World," written by Arthur Kent and Sylvia Dee, that was recorded by Skeeter Davis and popularized again by The Carpenters expressed my feelings exactly as it questioned why birds kept on singing when the world ended with the loss of a love.

I would wake up in the mornings hoping that it was a bad dream. Then I'd realize it wasn't. Phil was gone. How could I go on? But the sun still came up. Birds still sang. Cars still drove on the highways. Businesses kept running. The neighbors' dog kept pooping on my lawn . . . . The world kept going as if nothing had happened. But my world had crashed. I wanted to stop and scream, "How can you keep going? My husband died! Phil McElhaney died! Stop the world! We can't go on without him!"

People die. And the world keeps turning. I had to keep going. I'd always thought of myself as a strong, resilient woman. Someone who could survive life's challenges and make the best of whatever happened. I'm a glass-half-full person. I've been reading self-help books and studying positive mental attitude since my 20s. I'm someone who always looks on the bright side. Always looked for the silver lining. I've always believed that any challenge I faced only made me stronger and better positioned for whatever was next.

Not this time. This was something that would never turn out alright in the end. It was the end. The end of the life of the man I loved more than life itself. I wished it had been me. That I'd died instead of him.

There were many nights I prayed to God that I would die. That I could go on to be with Phil. This life held nothing for me without him. Every night I welcomed sleep and didn't want to wake up. Every morning I did wake up but I wasn't happy about it.

Mama didn't raise my sister and me to need a man. She raised us to be independent and self-sufficient. I'd lived alone for years before marrying.

Phil and I were born only one day apart and were thirty-four when we married. Neither of us had been married before. I knew intellectually that I could live alone and take care of myself but at the same time it didn't seem possible. My heart was broken. How could I possibly go on without him?

Why would I even want to?

Crying with a Professional

Not long after Phil had been diagnosed with a Stage IV Glioblastoma brain tumor and given only twelve to eighteen months to live, I began seeing a therapist. Dr. Robin Kirby is the best therapist I've ever had. And I've had a few! While some folks think therapy is for people with serious problems, I've always looked at therapy as a positive thing. Some people seek out a consultant to help them build a business or a coach to help them learn life skills or have better relationships. I think therapy helps us work toward becoming our best selves.

I began seeing Robin in order to process my feelings about Phil's diagnosis so that I could function as a caregiver. I couldn't take care of him if fear and sadness overwhelmed me and kept me immobilized.

"There is a team of doctors taking care of him," Robin would often say in our sessions. "For this one hour we're focusing totally on you."

Robin had helped me through accepting the diagnosis, facing each new obstacle in his treatment, and the progression of the disease. She'd helped me sort through my feelings and handle the stress of caregiving. It was natural for her to help me work through the grief too. I preferred the one-on-one sessions to going to a grief group. Normally I'm the one people come to when they need to talk. I listen and give advice and encouragement. Right now I just couldn't take listening to someone else's sorrow in addition to dealing with my own.

Time with Robin was one hour where I could sob, whine, and question "why me?" without being seen as weak and having family and friends think I was losing my mind. Some days I questioned my own sanity but Robin gave me a reality check and told me I'd survive.

"You're in pain," Robin said. "Pain won't kill you." Some days I believed her. Apparently 'pain killer' is a misnomer. Or is it an oxymoron?

Of course I had friends I could talk to. I'd been the strong shoulder for many of them as they went through job loss, divorce, and family craziness. I knew they would be there for me. But I didn't want to spend all my time with them sobbing and feeling sorry for myself. I didn't want to become the woman people avoided because she was always sad, depressed, crying, and moaning. I didn't want to wear them out. I knew they were sad and missed him too. I didn't want them to see me as wounded and broken. Not as wounded and broken as I really felt. I tried to appear "okay" for them. I was far from "okay."

With Robin I could sob and talk about the loss and loneliness that consumed me. I could bare my broken heart and my wounded spirit and know that it was a safe place to break down without it destroying me. I could do the ugly cry and not worry about my mascara running. She listened, gave good advice, and gave me assignments. She knew when I was being too hard on myself, and she called me on it when I was just being a baby. She taught me to have "pajama days" for rest but only one a week so I didn't disappear into the black hole of depression. She taught me to balance socializing with solitude. She helped me navigate the newness of being on my own again after years of marriage. She helped me know that despite my devastating grief I was normal and not going crazy. She gave me permission to grieve and nurture myself. She guided me in how to move forward in little baby steps until I was ready for bigger steps. Sometimes it was two steps forward and one step back. I am thankful that I didn't have to go it alone because the sadness was sometimes overwhelming.

Asking for Help

Just a month after Phil died I participated in a charity walk that was organized by some friends. I walked alongside Essie Escobedo, who owns Office Angels, a company that supplies administrative, accounting, and marketing help to entrepreneurs and small businesses. In the "how are you doing" conversation she asked what I was finding most challenging. Somehow I opened up to her and confessed something I hadn't told anyone else—my kitchen table was covered with unopened mail and unpaid bills.

Phil and I got a lot of mail. In addition to both of us working from home offices we had a couple real estate properties and various investments and we both subscribed to several magazines and papers. Mountains of mail!

I picked out the bills that had to be paid and dropped all the rest of the mail into a big shopping bag. Then it became multiple bags. Now it was all in a massive heap on the kitchen table.

Confusion and a lack of concentration are normal after an emotional trauma but it seemed I was admitting something horrifying. She didn't appear shocked at all. She said that when her dad died her mom was so distraught she couldn't even differentiate between bills and junk mail and needed help. Her sharing this normalized it enough so I could divulge that I was in the same situation.

I've always been independent and able to take care of myself. So I was embarrassed to admit that I couldn't even write out checks to pay bills. Even while I struggled to keep from falling apart, I just could not bear people thinking I wasn't strong enough to handle whatever came my way. Grief had taken me from bright and capable to befuddled and confused.

I used most of my energy to go out with friends and soak up the compassion and companionship that I desperately needed. I worked hard to appear "normal" then I came home exhausted from the effort it took to dress and go out to lunch, dinner, the bank, or grocery store. When I sat down to open the mail and pay the bills I just couldn't concentrate. It was overwhelming.

I would pick up a letter or bill, look at it, and put it down on the other side, moving things from one pile to another, unable to make sense of what I was looking at. Somehow I'd managed to keep the essential bills paid. The power and lights were still on and nothing had been repossessed!

I did forget to pay the mortgage for a month or two. The thought hit me one morning after paying bills. "Wait, we have a mortgage! How does that get paid if they don't send a bill?" Feeling sick in the pit of my stomach, I ran around frantically trying to figure it out. Was it being automatically deducted? Not according to the bank statements. "There must be a coupon book," I thought, running up to Phil's office to rummage through the drawers and files. It wasn't there. I looked in kitchen drawers. Even in bathroom drawers. Finally I found it in the night stand. Why the night stand I'll never know. I was a few months behind on paying it by now so I didn't know why I hadn't received any late notices. I grabbed the coupon book and headed out to the bank.

Through tears I confessed how during Phil's illness and death I'd forgotten all about the house payment and had come to settle it up. The nice young man voiced the obligatory, "I'm sorry for your loss," then listened politely without emotion or facial expression. He reached into a file behind him and pulled out a "hardship" form and began filling it out.

A hardship form. Of course.

Life has hardships and sometimes that means you can't pay your bills. Either you don't have the money or you've sort of lost your mind. Hardship. You just need a form. Missing payments seemed so irresponsible. But he made it seem so normal. The hardship form allowed the bank to forgive the late fees. To pardon my delinquent payment. Exoneration for being a half-crazed widow who's too addled to remember there was a mortgage.

I needed a hardship form for living.

It was too overwhelming to go through all the mail and see what should be filed and what could be trashed, much less determine any follow-up that may be needed. Let me just fill out a hardship form to make it all go away. Or get someone else to fill out the form since my mind had apparently turned to mush.

Back at home, Essie came to my rescue. She sat beside me at the table and tackled the mountain of mail. She placed bills that needed to be paid in piles according to business or personal. Things to be filed were in other stacks. Advertisements and solicitations were tossed. Information that could be read later was set aside. So simple when someone else did it.

Essie left with a six-inch deep plastic bin completely filled with medical bills and "explanation of benefits" (EOB) forms from the insurance company. And those were just what had accumulated in the past few months. That's how expensive cancer is. No wonder medical bills drive people to bankruptcy! Cancer doesn't just eat away at your life. It can destroy your finances and sanity, too.

One of Essie's Office Angels matched the EOB to the bills and called the hospital and doctor's offices to get the final balance for each account. This reduced the pile to only an inch of medical bills that had to be paid. She helped break the overwhelming mess down to manageable chunks that I could handle.

If you have a serious physical trauma you may have visible injuries like cuts, broken bones, gaping wounds, or missing limbs. If someone sees you limping or with your arm in a sling it makes sense that you may need help with your normal routine. When your trauma is emotional the wounds don't always show. You may be crying, depressed, tired, and confused. You may have an inability to concentrate and a fuzzy memory. Somehow we don't allow ourselves the same compassion in needing help with our routines. Fortunately, I had a therapist to remind me to cut myself some slack.

Distractions

Being self-employed, I put my work aside to be with Phil while he was sick. The good news was that immediately after he died I didn't have anyone to answer to, no expectations, nowhere I had to be. The bad news was that I didn't have anyone to answer to, no expectations, nowhere I had to be. No real reason to crawl out of bed.

Some days I didn't.

Like anyone who has suffered emotional trauma, I needed more than the usual rest and sleep. Death also brings paperwork with probating a will, changing names on accounts, receiving and distributing death certificates, and so much more. Great distractions that took a lot of emotional energy but still left a lot of hours to fill. Lots of time to be overwhelmed with sadness.

Trying to fill those hours with eating just created other problems. I did a lot of grief therapy with Ben & Jerry. Both while Phil was very sick and after he passed. It was way too easy to calm my anxieties late at night with a pint of ice cream. (That's a single serving, right?) When my sister was there she easily became my partner in crime. We'd watch *Biggest Loser* while binging on New York Chocolate Chunk. Crack in a cup. Of course we just ate it right out of the carton. So that would be crack in a carton.

One Saturday morning I walked into the kitchen and found Cynthia standing at the coffee pot, her hands clasping a steaming cup of coffee, a somber look on her face. "Myra, we have to break up with Ben & Jerry," she said. "It's an abusive relationship." The possessiveness of a pint as a single serving was followed by guilt and shame. Control. (Craving) Denial. (What? A pint isn't a single serving?) Humiliation. (Can't believe I ate a whole pint! Again.) Guilt. (I should not have done that.) Then back to craving. We needed to break the cycle.

I learned to look for healthy distractions and discovered them in my friends. We went to lunch, dinner, events, walks, shopping. Anything to distract me from my pain and devastation for a little while. We would briefly do the "how are you" update from me, then I'd get them to talk about work, their families, or anything that wasn't death, illness, cancer, hospitals, or funerals. Of course we talked about Phil. We laughed and shared memories. We talked about things he said or did and imagined what he'd think or say if he were here. He was almost always with us in spirit in those early days. Talking about his life felt good. Talking about his death didn't so we avoided that. Then I'd go home and face the emptiness. The reality that he wasn't there. That he never would be again.

To fill the emptiness, I began watching movies or reading in bed before going to sleep. Soon after Phil's funeral my friend, Jean, handed me a book and said, "If you need a distraction this may work." It was *My Horizontal Life* by Chelsea Handler. Jean was right! I usually read business and self-help books. Reading this hilarious memoir of the famous bad girl and her "sexcapades" got my mind off my own personal trauma. And made me think about sex. But I wasn't having sex. Maybe I should go back to Ben & Jerry.

I began reading fiction again and spent many weekends curled in my "reading chair" with a romance or cozy mystery. Someone recommended *Good Grief* by Lolly Winston. The main character is Sophie Stanton, a young woman who has just been widowed. The book follows her in the first year after dealing with her husband's death. At one point she was struggling to return to her high-pressure executive position. In the depths of despair, but knowing she needed to be there for an important project, she showed up to work in bathrobe and bunny slippers. That made me laugh!

It also gave me something to measure against. Many days I was one step away from wearing my bathrobe and bunny slippers in public. The story helped me to see someone else struggling after a loss like mine but going on with her life. Eventually. The author had written the book after losing her father but she was right on target with the feelings of a widow. Right down to the bunny slippers.

The problem with movies was that somebody always died in them. Under other circumstances I probably wouldn't have noticed the prevalence of death but my sensitivity was heightened.

Years ago I heard a story of an old man who had lost his wife. Friends and relatives looked on sympathetically as he sat on the porch alone, distraught. Soon a little boy went over to the man and crawled up in his lap. They sat huddled together for a while before they came back into the house together. The old man seemed to feel better.

Someone asked the boy, "What did you say to him?"

"Nothing," the little boy replied. "I just helped him cry."

The movies helped me cry. I would crawl in bed with a sad movie and a box of tissues. It might seem morbid but it was like cleaning a wound. It seemed to relieve some of the pain.

One movie I watched over and over is *P.S. I Love You* with Hillary Swank. It's about a young woman who loses her husband to a brain tumor. Too close to home, right? How could I watch a movie about what I'd just experienced? But again, it helped me to heal.

The main character, Holly (played by Hilary Swank), starts out distraught and unable to function in her life. At one point, when she hasn't left the house for days, her mother and sisters come in and find her dancing around the house in her husband's shirt. I found comfort in wearing Phil's clothes in those early days too. And using his Old Spice body wash so I'd be surrounded with his smell.

One night I had an anxiety attack. I'd been straightening out the clothes in his side of the closet. Flipping through them as if looking for something to wear. I just wanted to be with his clothes because that was as close as I could get to being with him. I'd look at each shirt, jacket, pair of pants and remember how he looked in it. I'd remember him wearing them when we'd gone someplace or done something special. I rearranged his shoes. I kept them very neat, not ready to accept that he wasn't coming back and would never need them again.

That night I woke in a panic knowing that the sweater that went with one of the shirts wasn't in the closet. I flipped through the shirts and jackets, over and over, trying to find it. I finally found it folded in a drawer in the chest. Relieved, I could sleep again. Hugging his sweater to my heart.

In another scene from the movie, Holly's mother tells her she can't go on with the Miss Havisham routine. Remember Miss Havisham from Dickens's *Great Expectations*? The spinster falls in love and is swindled out of her fortune by the man she is to marry. He sends a letter to call off the wedding and she wanders around the decaying mansion wearing her wedding dress and one shoe. The cake is rotting on the table and the clock stops at the time the letter arrived. Sometimes I really related to Miss Havisham. Wandering around in my big house, not wanting anything to change. Keeping Phil's clothes in place. Not wanting time to move forward.

By the end of the movie and Holly's first year as a widow, she'd found her way and was hopeful. I liked that it didn't end with a romance. It showed she was open to the possibility but she was strong as a woman alone and would be okay with or without a husband. The feminist in me loved that ending. The widow in me found it hopeful.

Reading was one of the more positive ways I found distraction. While I was aware of not giving in too much to "the devil liquor," as my friend, June Cline's other half, Jerry, calls it, I did do a little grief therapy with Jose over the first year. It's not uncommon for people who've been through a trauma, death, or divorce to hit the bottle a little harder afterward.

Like most southern girls, I grew up with a gallon jug full of tea in the refrigerator at all times. After Phil died I replaced that with a gallon jug of Margaritas. You never know when you'll need one!

Cynthia hadn't had a drink since her son was born twenty years earlier and had preferred frozen drinks back in her single days. It wasn't long until she had adopted my preference for a "Texas margarita, on the rocks with salt." Especially with the gallon jug always handy, right in the fridge.

We had a regular Friday night routine of Mexican food and margaritas. Her son, Christopher, was twenty years old—not yet drinking age—so he became our designated driver. It was a good fit. From the time he was a little boy, Christopher loved cars and tractors. As a toddler he'd some- times say, "Let's go to Papa's. I want to drive something!" In the country he could drive the riding lawn mower or tractor way before being old enough to handle a car. He was a calm, responsible teenager and at twenty (still teenager-ish) he actually preferred driving to drinking.

I was such a good influence on my sister and nephew. Ha!

Sometimes I did overindulge. Since we were the party house for our friends, I had several parties during my first year of widowhood. Gathering our friends around me and telling "Phil stories" made me feel closer to him. We'd always end up in the Irish pub in our basement that was Phil's pride and joy. It had been the last home project he'd completed just BD (Before Diagnosis). He enjoyed many parties and football games there the last couple years and we always sensed his spirit in the pub.

Our friend, Mike, who was one of Phil's racquetball buddies, was always ready to cheer me up. He apparently thought tequila shots would be good fun for livening up the party. Never one to shy away from tequila shots, I participated enthusiastically. Too enthusiastically.

Before all the guests were gone, Cynthia noticed I was missing and found me in the master bath praying to the porcelain god. She'd never seen me drunk before, let alone puking my guts out. Without saying a word, she leaned against the sink and watched to make sure I was safe. There wasn't much she could do but it did feel better knowing she was there.

My neighbor, Elaine, soon came in. Apparently her college years had given her more experience with this particular malady. She came right over and held my hair back. I'd always heard of the kind of friend that'd hold your hair when you upchucked but I'd managed to live to the ripe old age of 51 without ever needing it. As soon as I finished she got a cool, wet cloth for my head and asked Cynthia for my nightgown. They started undressing me and put me in some pajama top or T-shirt they'd found. Elaine (did I mention her experience?) put me into bed, propped pillows under my head, turned me onto my side, and put my arms around a small trash can that was positioned to capture any other retching.

Yep, grief therapy with Jose Cuervo. Pain multiplied. I was officially pathetic! Damn, Devil Liquor!

Gratitude

For many years BD (Before Diagnosis) I practiced gratitude. It's easy for us to list things in general we are grateful for, but when you make gratitude a practice you begin to look for things to be grateful for in every day, in any situation.

Many times during Phil's illness my gratitude list for the day included skilled surgeons, caring nurses, and modern medicines. After Phil passed I made a point to continue my gratitude practice. I was fortunate to have lots of friends, a supportive family, and a caring mother-in-law, and to be in a financial situation where I didn't have to worry about whether I could support myself without him. Despite my personal tragedy of losing the love of my life, I was still richly blessed.

In even the darkest days I could find something to be thankful for. The day the tumor was found I had rushed Phil to the ER and the waiting room was practically empty so they got him in right away. That's unheard of! Then I was distraught while he was having tests and one of the ER nurses was so comforting and supportive to me.

The day of his brain surgery my mother was able to be at the hospital with me so I wasn't alone. The doctor called sooner than expected to tell me that the surgery had gone well and Phil was ready for me to come to his room.

All the time Phil and I got to spend together during his treatment, while he was feeling okay but couldn't travel for work as he usually did, allowed us to grow even stronger in our love and enjoy the cuddling and hanging out together.

The day Phil died friends were there surrounding me with support. My sister came as soon as she heard and stayed with me until after the burial.

Even in the midst of my sorrow there were always things for which to be thankful. I'm so glad I knew to look for them.

An Inappropriate Widow

"You are hereby notified that a warrant has been issued for your arrest."

I read and re-read the letter. Only a week after my husband was buried there was a warrant out for my arrest. How could this be? I'd always been an upstanding, law-abiding citizen. Well, except for a little issue with my lead foot. Occasionally, okay, frequently, I do break a speeding law or two.

Guess I'd forgotten about the last time. A few months before Phil went into the hospital I'd driven him to Chattanooga to attend some work meetings and travel for a few days with his engineer, Steve. Phil couldn't drive due to the possibility of seizures but he was still able to work from home and call on customers with Steve when he was feeling up to it and we could work it around his treatment schedule. The last time I took him to meet Steve I got a speeding ticket on the way home.

During the last three months of Phil's life, he spent forty-two days in the hospital. That included two 911 calls, two ambulance rides, two passes through ER, two stints in neuro-ICU and almost three weeks in rehab. Then he came home and was on in-home care for three weeks, then hospice for a week. Add to that, a constant stream of family, friends and healthcare workers. When he died there were multiple overnight guests during the funeral, followed by burial in his home state of Tennessee.

Yeah, I had a few things on my mind. I forgot about the ticket. Cherokee County didn't forget!

They weren't messing around either from the looks of the "You are hereby notified of a bench warrant for your arrest" letter. I could just imagine the Cherokee County Sheriff screaming into the neighborhood with sirens blaring, dragging the widow McElhaney out to the squad car in handcuffs. The neighbors would be abuzz with rumors about my crime. They'd suspect I'd somehow been responsible for my husband's death. The deadly brain tumor caper.

A bench warrant for my arrest. Just what every grieving widow needs!

I called Ted. Ted is my B.F.I.L. (Best-Friend-In-Law.) He was Phil's best friend and the best man at our wedding. Now he's the one I turn to for advice. Ted always seems to know what to do or knows a guy who'll know.

Ted got a real kick out of hearing that "the widow" was now a fugitive from justice. Sure enough, he knew a guy who knew a couple of the judges in Cherokee County. He got the fellow to call their offices. Since it was

Friday afternoon, they'd already left for the day. Ted called back saying, "Do not drive that car this weekend. The warrant will be connected to the license plate and if you're stopped this weekend they'll take you to jail." He then gave me a stern warning to be at the courthouse first thing Monday morning.

Then he joked, "Now have fun this weekend but stay out of jail."

Fortunately, my cousin Melany was coming to spend the weekend. She had to drive anywhere we went during her visit. Now I'd led her into a life of crime with harboring a fugitive and assisting me in evading arrest.

In olden times widows were supposed to wear black mourning attire and go into seclusion or at least limit social engagements and visitors for the first year. I never intended to be a widow. Now that I was, I certainly didn't care about being an appropriate one!

By Monday morning I'd figured out that maybe instead of driving to the courthouse first thing, I could just call. The woman who answered the phone listened as I played the "widow card" for the first time. I told my story of forgetting the ticket during my husband's illness, hospitalization, hospice care, and death. She gave the obligatory, "I'm sorry for your loss," then changed the court date and removed the warrant. I was free to drive again. Just not as fast.

When my new court date rolled around my teenage grand-nephew was visiting so I took him along to traffic court. You can always serve as a bad example, right?

Baby Steps Forward

Losing my husband was devastating. My world seemed off-balance and I was emotionally fragile. Yet I was surrounded with friends, had lots to be grateful for, and could still find humor in most situations. I was slowly and cautiously moving forward. Even with a broken heart.

Widows and widowers are often told they aren't moving forward fast enough or that they're moving too fast. Some talk of not knowing when or how to move forward. I think the first time after the funeral that you are out of bed, dressed, and stepping outside your door you are moving forward. How far and how fast is very personal and there will be setbacks along the way.

Underneath the hurt, sadness, grief, and my Miss Havisham moments I knew there was a pilot light of determination. I promised myself that although I'd had tragedy in my life, I would not allow my life to become a tragedy.

• • •

CHAPTER 2

You Talking to Me?

"It ain't gonna be so easy from the start . . . ."

As I turned the key and started the car, Elton John's lyrics spoke to me from the radio. Specifically to ME!

It was my first time to drive in about a week. Elton John had been Phil's favorite singer so we listened to him a lot and saw him in concert. I had never heard this song before. I have never heard it since. It truly seemed as if Phil was using Elton John's lyrics to speak to me. This type of incident is referred to as an "after death communication" (ADC). Hearing personal messages in the lyrics of a song is a common example.

"If I can contact you, I will," Phil said to me one day in the early days of his diagnosis. He was totally somber. I'd always joked and been irreverent about death and the afterlife. Phil was not one to make vague promises or joke about things like that. I was fascinated by stories of people who had seen ghosts or received messages from the beyond. I'd visited psychics, read about past lives, and even did a little research on near death experiences when assigned by a magazine to do a story on a woman who'd had one. Phil had never seemed interested in any of these things. Now to say this out of the blue after a cancer diagnosis surprised me. His promise stood out in my memory. I believe the lyrics on the radio that day were my first ADC from Phil. Many others followed in the first couple years after his death. One day I was driving on a curvy, narrow highway in the country near where I grew up. As I rounded a curve a truck was pulling out of a driveway and apparently didn't see me. Without thinking, I swerved to miss him and accelerated. He barely missed hitting me broadside! Just as I passed him I heard the words on the radio loud and clear, "I'll be there for you . . ." the Jon Bon

Jovi song was playing. "Words can't say what love can do . . ." It seemed as if Phil was telling me that he was protecting me. Accelerating to avoid a collision isn't a "Myra move." I'd most likely hit the brakes. Accelerating is a "Phil move."

Black Butterflies

Phil drove a green Infinity Q45 that had over 100,000 miles on it. He loved that car! He called it "The Q." His boss called it the green bomb. The guys he worked with kidded him about driving a car with so many miles on it. He loved it so much that it was the second Infinity Q45 he'd owned. Both green! He thought they were well made, dependable, smart-looking, and comfortable for someone who drove as much for work as he did. He bought both cars when they were a couple years old and maintained them faithfully.

When Phil died he had The Q and an old Nissan pickup that he used for hauling stuff. I had my dream car—a classic 1988 Mercedes 560 SL convertible. Red. I loved that car! However, I did not need two cars and a truck. I decided to get rid of all three and buy one newer-model car. I dreaded getting rid of Phil's car.

The day the men came to pick it up I was sad and wondering if I was doing the right thing. As the guy walked around the car, checking it out before taking it, I stood in the doorway of the garage watching. A big black butterfly flew toward the front of the car. Then it flew right to me, almost flying into me. It circled back and forth from the car to me. I didn't remember ever seeing a black butterfly before and thought it odd that it would fly so close to me. When they started to leave, I walked back into the house to watch from the front door as The Q left for the last time. I couldn't believe my eyes when the black butterfly was now outside the front door.

I went to my computer and searched for the symbolism of a black butterfly. I learned that in some cultures it's believed that a black butterfly signifies the spirit of a recently deceased person showing their presence and approval. Amazing! I claimed it as a sign that Phil approved of letting go of The Q.

Pennies from Heaven

Another common ADC is pennies or coins showing up in unexpected places. Phil collected his change. He had penny banks of various shapes and sizes. Quarters in one. Dimes in another. Nickels in another. I used to tease him about the jars of money everywhere. After he died I continued to find change in unexpected places all around the house. My sister and I began to joke about Phil's change everywhere. I soon noticed that when I was doing something new and fun I would often find a penny.

I went to a writing conference for my birthday and when I parked at the cottage where I would stay I opened the door to find a penny on the ground right where I was about to step. When I purchased my new car there was a penny on the floor. This type of thing happened often. One day I told one of Phil's friends about it. He said, "Come on, Phil, you can do better than a penny!" The next day I went to show some friends the high-rise I'd soon call home. When I stopped in the circle drive in front of the building and opened the door, there was a dime! Ha! What a sense of humor Phil had!

Electronics

"I think I'm getting messages from the beyond," I told Ted one day.

"Beyond where?" he asked.

I explained that my car was in the shop, my computer had died, and my phone was acting up. "I think Phil wants me to get a new car, computer, and phone." I laughed.

"Maybe he wants you to stay home, get off the internet, and stop talking on the phone," he countered. Funny guy.

It's common for lights and electronics to go out or act up around the death of a loved one. The year after Phil died it seemed that we were constantly replacing light bulbs and the lights often flickered.

Visitations and Dreams

It's not uncommon for people to feel the presence of a recently deceased loved one or to smell their fragrance. Maybe a favorite cologne or pipe tobacco.

I awoke early one morning to the slight shaking of the bed. It felt like someone sat on the bed right next to me and placed a hand on my side to comfort me. I opened my eyes and no one was there. This is also a common type of ADC.

Sometimes people who have passed show up in dreams. Sometimes it's so real you feel as if they are actually there with you. This is referred to as a visitation. Phil's friend and motorcycle riding buddy, Spencer, occasionally calls or emails to tell me Phil has visited him in a dream. Phil rides up on his bike, talks for a bit, and then rides off.

Dream interpretation has always interested me and I read a couple books on the subject years ago.

"What is the emotion you feel in the dream?" Dr. Stephen Preas, a psychiatrist friend, once asked when we were discussing dreams. "Ask yourself where in your life you are feeling that emotion."

Those questions have been more helpful to me than anything I've read when I want to determine what a dream is trying to tell me.

I've only had a few dreams of Phil since his death and while they weren't scary, they weren't exactly comforting. In one, he was telling me that he was leaving me. We had a good marriage and although all relationships have times that are challenging we never considered or discussed separating. I awoke from this dream very upset. When I asked myself the questions about what emotion it brought up and where that was present in my life, I realized that Phil had left me through his death. I think the dream was supposed to help me to accept that.

Most of the ADC's were comforting, as if Phil was watching over me and showing his approval or protecting me. The dreams made me feel as if he was telling me to move on. Each helpful in its own way as I navigated adjusting to life without him.

Are You a Believer?

You may not believe in after-death communications. Many people don't. That's okay too. I read a book by a woman who had lost a son and talked of looking for signs everywhere. Her fundamental religious beliefs didn't allow for the possibility of loved ones sending signs from heaven. She said that what we see as signs are just our own justifications because we need so desperately to believe that they are still with us. Maybe so. Are there really messages from the other side? Or are they our own inventions for our own comfort? I don't think it matters. If you see something as a sign and it gives you comfort or brings a smile to your face then that's enough for me.

My friend Mark rolled his eyes when I told him about this stuff. He's not a believer. Then one night he was helping me with some work around the house and spent the night in the downstairs guest room. He couldn't wait to tell me the next morning that the ceiling fan had come on all by itself.

"I thought Phil was telling me something," he said, "Then I realized I'd sat on the remote control."

To paraphrase Sigmund Freud, sometimes a ceiling fan is just a ceiling fan.

I've asked others who lost spouses, parents, or close friends if they have similar experiences. Most have. It tends to happen more in the first year after death. The people I've talked with find the experiences comforting and helpful as they learn to let go. And I treasured each little sign that Phil's spirit was still with me.

It's been a few years and they don't happen much anymore. I miss them.

Do the spirits of our loved ones stay around us for a while and send comforting signs? No one knows for sure. You get to choose what you believe. I believe they sometimes give us signs. I believe that although the person is gone, their love is with you forever.

• • •

I believe that although the
person is gone, their love
is with you forever.

Myra McElhaney

My God, My God;
Why Hast Thou Forsaken Me?

When I told my therapist I'd lost my faith after my husband's illness and death, she said, "Even Jesus cried out from the cross, 'My God, my God! Why hast thou forsaken me?' So why wouldn't you feel that God has abandoned you?" It wasn't really a question. "This is what I call getting real with God," she continued.

I believe that there is much we don't know about how God works and what is on the other side of this life. I've come to be okay with not knowing. I believe, as the old hymn says, "we'll understand it better by and by."

Many of the spiritual leaders I'd read and followed teach that you can create the life you want. That your thoughts, energy, and faith can attract into your life whatever you desire. Some call this prosperity gospel or new age "secrets." It agrees with the Bible verses about "ask and ye shall receive" and teachings of having faith as a grain of mustard seed.

Spiritual Practice BD (Before Diagnosis)

Prior to Phil's diagnosis I felt more spiritual and closer to God than I ever had in my life. This will be news to many of my friends and family. After having grown up in a strict, fundamentalist church where even the way I dressed set me apart from others, now my spirituality is very personal. Not something I publicize. I don't attend church and I know some think you can't be close to God while "forsaking the gathering together" as is mentioned in the Bible (Hebrews 10:25). But I pray daily, meditate, read spiritual books, and focus on growing my personal relationship with God as I understand God to be. At least I did before Phil died.

My spirituality was a daily practice. I was focused, prayed, meditated, maintained a practice of gratitude, and read inspirational readings daily. I truly felt that I was, to use fundamental Christian terminology, "in the center of God's will." And we had a plan.

A grand plan. Every morning at my desk I pulled out my sheet of affirmations, statements of my vision for the various aspects of my life—spiritual, marriage, business, personal, health, and social. I fully believed that I was living God's plan for my life. My spiritual life was a top priority and (however it may have looked from the outside to anyone judging spirituality based on church attendance, abstinence, and Bible-thumping) I was in a very spiritual place in my life. I was writing a book and sensed that it was more than my work. It was a calling. A work God had guided me to through prayer and meditation.

Then with the tumor diagnosis it all went to hell in a hand basket.

I kept meditating and praying by Phil's bedside or wherever we were. I kept practicing gratitude daily, giving thanks for all the good that was there even on the darkest days. I was praying for a miracle and had faith it would be received.

Faith as a Grain of Mustard Seed

I remembered as a little girl that I would read and reread the words of Jesus underlined in my Bible. Matthew, Chapter 17, Verse 20 of the King James Version says: "If ye have faith as a grain of mustard seed, ye shall say unto this mountain, Remove hence to yonder place and it shall remove; and nothing shall be impossible unto you." As a kid I would open my Bible to this verse and pray my little heart out, begging God to honor his promise and answer my prayers because I had faith. I didn't pray this way for little things but for big things like Daddy coming home safely when he was late from work or for my friend to be saved.

From childhood I cried out to a God who answered my prayers. I had faith. I may have become more liberal in my beliefs and ways of worship but I always had faith. When Phil was first diagnosed I didn't want people who heard about his illness to think he was dying and write him off with "ain't it awful." I wanted them to pray with faith.

We chose not to tell even our own families that the doctors had said he had only twelve to eighteen months to live. I didn't want that thought in anybody's head. We discussed that we'd focus on the possibilities, not the prognosis. I believe in miracles and I believed Phil would live one.

In the face of statistical data and medical information I believed with my whole heart that he would survive. I set up a CaringBridge blog where I'd report what we were doing and what was going on with us. While I would talk about doctor's appointments and changes in treatment, I purposefully kept the blog positive and upbeat. I reported every morsel of good news and omitted some of the bad. I didn't want the hundreds of family and friends who came there for updates to give up on him. I wanted them to pray with faith.

I know that when you hear such a frightening diagnosis as "brain tumor" you instantly see someone in a hospital bed dying. I posted photos of Phil and what we were doing in our lives. Photos of us with friends, at restaurants, concerts, and snow skiing. I went to the gym with him and took photos of him and "the boys" playing racquetball. I wanted everyone who visited the blog to see that he was LIVING! He was living with a brain tumor. Not dying from one. We kept the positive messages up so well that the Physician's Assistant at the radiation oncologist's office often used him as an example to her newly diagnosed patients. "Don't give up! I've got a patient playing racquetball every day," she'd tell them.

After his brain surgery to remove the first tumor I posted pre-op photos of the sensors on his head to guide the surgeon and post-op photos of him smiling beside the pool with the huge scar down the left side of his head. Friends sometimes commented at how he'd so amazingly "kicked cancer's butt." No one believed he was dying. Especially not me. I prayed with faith that the cancer would be held at bay. People all across the country prayed with faith that he'd recover.

Hey, we weren't even asking for a cure. Just that the tumor wouldn't grow so he could continue to live his life. After all, this was Phil McElhaney. In almost seventeen years of marriage I could count on one hand the times he'd been sick. Even with a cold. And as our friend Susan Garrard said when she heard the initial diagnosis, "Nothing can happen to Phil. He's the sun the rest of us revolve around!"

Not long after Phil's surgery, Senator Ted Kennedy was diagnosed with the same type of tumor. Glioblastoma Multiforme, Stage 4. The baddest, deadliest brain tumor known to man. With all his money and contacts Ted Kennedy called in the top neurosurgeons in the country for consultations. He chose the same guy who had done Phil's surgery only weeks earlier.

Dr. Allan H. Friedman, an internationally recognized tumor and vascular neurosurgeon, was program director of Neurosurgery for Duke University's Preston Robert Tisch Brain Tumor Center. He also did the brain surgery for Tug McGraw, father of singer Tim McGraw who wrote the song "Live Like You're Dying" about his father's illness.

The rock star of brain surgeons. The cutting edge, experimental treatment from one of the leading brain tumor centers in the country. A healthy body. Determination. Thousands of family, friends, friends of friends, and prayer groups across the country praying with faith. Nope. My husband was not dying. There are inexplicable medical miracles. I believed with my whole heart that Phil would be one. Possibilities, not prognosis!

During the last month I was praying hard during the night when Phil was in neuro ICU and the words, "total and complete recovery" popped into my mind. It was as if someone had said them to me. I held on to that as a promise I believed was from God. Phil's doctors had said that he could recover from the damage of the seizures and regain the abilities he'd had before. Of course they never made any promises regarding the cancer but as long as the tumor didn't grow he could regain his ability to walk and communicate. Like someone recovering from a stroke. I held on tightly to that belief and the words "total and complete recovery." I truly believed that he would regain his abilities and continue to live as the new and evolving experimental medications kept the tumor at bay. I believed this with all my heart, soul, and mind.

I believed this right up until the time the oncologist pulled me from Phil's bedside, showed me the new brain scans with signs of tumor growth in multiple places, and told me there was nothing else he could do.

Phil's seizures had left him with receptive aphasia. That means he could talk but couldn't understand what was being said to him . . . the communicating and understanding are different parts of the brain. For example, if he was cold he could say, "I'm cold," yet if you asked if he was cold he couldn't understand the words. It was like you were speaking a foreign language. This made it difficult to communicate.

Although I told him what the doctors said there was no way of knowing for sure what or how much he understood. He didn't reply.

I closed the door to the hospital room, crawled in bed with him, and we lay there listening to his favorite music. "What A Wonderful World" by Louis Armstrong was playing while we lay there knowing our wonderful world was coming to an end. Phil still needed me. Although he couldn't communicate and I didn't know how much he understood we held each other tightly as tears rolled down my cheeks.

From that day forward I took Phil home and spent all my time and energy caring for him as the illness took away his life. Bit by bit.

I was with him constantly except when friends or family came to give me a short break. He wasn't able to walk or move himself from bed to chair to wheelchair so I assisted with lifting and pivoting him into position. I handled bathing, dressing, giving medications and feeding him. The last few days of his life I didn't get out of the house and rarely left his bedside other than getting his food or medicine from the kitchen and going to the bathroom.

I didn't have the time or energy to argue with God then. Plus I had Shock, Denial, Xanax, and Prozac to help me cope.

And then Phil died.

God, I Thought We Talked?

When things don't turn out right and go according to plan, my friend, June Cline, often looks up to the sky and says kiddingly, "God, I thought we talked?"

That's the way I felt when Phil was diagnosed and even more after he died.

Before Phil was diagnosed he was top salesman in the country for his company. I was working on a book that I truly believed I'd been inspired by God to write. Years of work on the book had finally culminated in my finding an agent in New York who was already talking to prospective publishers about buying it. I was about to click "SEND" on the final information to her when Phil was diagnosed.

What about me, God? What about the book you wanted me to write? What about the plan we had? Why Phil? Why me?

How could God not honor my faith? How could he not honor the prayers of my mother and Phil's mother? They are godly women who go to church every Sunday morning, Sunday night, and Wednesday night prayer meeting. What about the hundreds of people across the country? There were people with that "old time religion" calling his name in their prayer groups. Catholics were praying the rosary. New-age believers were sending light, love, and angels. Positive mental attitude advocates were visualizing him fully healed. His hairdresser from the islands had sent healing concoctions for him to drink and Holy Water to anoint him with.

Faith that could move mountains and the best in modern medicine. How could God let him die? I was so mad at God. Everyone else had done all they could. God let us down. Where was our miracle?

Most people who knew me probably expected me to delve right back into my business and finish writing the book once Phil died. I didn't. If God wasn't holding up his side of the bargain, I wasn't doing anything. Not a thing.

Daddy used to tell a joke about an old man who was so lazy he lay down under a tree and said, "Come breath, go breath. I ain't a gonna draw ye." Too lazy to breath. That's what I felt like doing. Good thing breathing is automatic.

They say that anger is one of the stages of grief. (Author Elisabeth Kubler-Ross first outlined the five stages of grief in her book *On Death and Dying* in 1969.) Sometimes people are angry at the person for dying. Especially if the person died due to something they did or something they could have prevented. Sometimes the bereaved are mad that the death leaves them in an undesirable predicament. Sometimes they are mad at people around them because of circumstances surrounding the death or their handling of arrangements. I was just mad at God. Mad that he took my husband. The one person I loved most in the world. The finest person I knew. God let cancer take him from me.

Phil was a man of integrity. A good man. Successful, smart, kind, helpful to others, healthy, athletic, decent in every way, loved by everyone. He was dead and Charles Manson is still alive. Pure evil, rotting away in prison for thirty years. But my husband gets a deadly brain tumor and dies at the age of fifty-one. What the hell is up with that?

Thank God there are therapists! So my therapist, Robin, said it's not uncommon or sinful to be mad at God. To "get real with God" about feelings. "God can take it," she said.

I was mad for a long time.

Spiritual Surrender

I called my friend Jennifer Bristol about 11:30 one night. We'd been friends for years and she lived nearby. I'd come home to find my garage door opened. Without the kitchen door locked that gave free access to the house. I weighed my options. I could go in, search the house, and risk surprising burglars, or I could call the cops. Neither seemed like a good option.

I didn't want the police to come screaming into the neighborhood only to give me a dismissing look after finding nothing amiss inside. I didn't want to lie awake all night wondering if murderers were hiding in the attic waiting to kill me in my sleep. I didn't want to go in and face seeing missing TV's and stuff if someone had looted the place. I just wanted to go to sleep.

Jennifer answered, "I'm in bed."

"Can I come spend the night?" I told her the situation and she said to come on over.

As I lay in bed in her guest room I began to pray for God to protect me and the house. This prayer had brought me comfort so many times before as I placed my worries into God's hands. Realizing that my prayers for Phil's life and health hadn't been answered I literally said aloud, "Do whatever you want to, God. You're going to anyway." I rolled over and went to sleep.

That's something Mama used to say when I asked for advice she knew I wouldn't take. She didn't mean it. I guess I didn't either. I'd just lost faith that God would answer my prayers.

In all spiritual teachings there is talk of surrender. Giving your will over to God. Letting go of outcomes. I thought I understood and had done that. But I hadn't really until that moment. We often pray "Thy will be done" and yet hold on to it being done our way. At that moment I just gave in to knowing that whatever happened would happen and I'd do whatever I had to do to survive. Or not survive. The great spiritual "Whatever!"

I always thought spiritual surrender was supposed to feel like handing an issue over to God. Reverent. For me it was more like a loud deep sigh. Resignation. Whatever it was, I could relax and go to sleep. Whatever happened I'd just deal with it tomorrow.

As I'm writing this I have a Pandora classical music channel playing in the background. Right this minute they're playing, "He Whispers Sweet Peace to Me." I recognize it from church singing during my childhood. The lyrics express how, ". . . when misgivings darken the day and faith's light I cannot see . . ." that God gives peace. I was looking for peace that night and it came in the form of surrender. Just letting go and not being attached to the outcome.

"I've stopped talking to God," I told June weeks later when she asked how I was doing.

"How's that working for ya?" she asked in her best Dr. Phil imitation.

"Fine," I answered. "He's still running the Universe and I've stopped telling him how."

I'd lost my faith about having my prayers answered and being given what I want or ask for. I found faith in my ability to handle whatever comes my way. I was okay with letting God figure out what that'd be.

Praying Again

I found it very difficult to pray. No wonder, given my lack of faith situation.

Soon I began to miss my spiritual time of daily reading, prayer, and meditation. I missed feeling close to God. When I would start to pray words would fail me. I guess I didn't realize how much of our prayers, mine at least, are prayers of supplication. Although I always start my prayers with thanksgiving I didn't realize how much I really used praying to ask for something. To pray for Phil's health and healing BDD (before diagnosis/death), to pray for protection for him, for my family, and friends. For guidance. For faith. For help with whatever I was facing.

Other denominations and religions have written or formal prayers that are recited. Catholics pray the rosary. I once attended an Episcopal funeral where they did lots of reciting and responsive reading. It was the longest funeral I'd ever attended but I could easily see how the rituals of reciting and reading were comforting. Sort of providing a structure around the grieving.

Since I found it difficult to pray I occasionally just recited the Lord's Prayer. Even that asks for stuff. Daily bread, forgiveness, and protection from temptation and delivery from evil. But the words seemed empty. I also began listening to CDs with other people's prayers. Marianne Williamson does beautiful prayers. I heard her speak in person once and was very touched by her thoughtful, loving, and generous prayers.

I also went back to a sort of prayer formula that I'd come up with years earlier. It's a 5-step prayer: 1. Gratitude. 2. Forgiveness 3. Release. 4. Love 5. Guidance.

First, I gave thanks for everything that came to mind for the day or around the situation. Second I searched my mind to see who, if anyone, I needed to forgive for any real or perceived slight. Next I released any anxiety, tension, confusion, fear, jealousy, or any negative feeling, energy or emotion around my situation or in general. Then I prayed to be filled with God's love. As I asked to be filled with love I visualized love like sunlight pouring into me from above and imagine it filling every cell and fiber of my being. Then I prayed to be surrounded with love, sort of like a love filter, so that every thought, word, action I had would be filtered through love before going out to another. Likewise, every thought, word, and action of others would be filtered through love before reaching me.

Praying this way always left me feeling close to God and spiritually centered. But during this painful time of my life I didn't feel centered or sassy (my often snarky, smart-mouthed self). Mostly I felt broken. I'd been robbed of the person I loved most in life and of the life we had. I felt betrayed by God. Abandoned.

At least with a lifetime of spirituality I could rest assured that God doesn't get mad or punish people for losing faith. God doesn't have human characteristics. Me being mad at God was like a fish being mad at the ocean. I could just let my wounds heal and know the universe wouldn't fall apart because I wasn't praying.

My beliefs and understanding of God did not change. I just lost faith in having my prayers answered. So I stopped asking for anything. I just kept feeling gratitude for what I had each day.

Meister Eckhart says, "If the only prayer you ever say in your entire life is thank you, it will be enough."

I learned to be at peace with what is. To be okay with questions that have no answers. To face the unknown without feeling I need to control life. I was stronger in knowing I could survive what seemed unsurvivable. Maybe that's what faith was really all about.

Some people go deeper in their faith after losing a spouse. Some turn away or embrace a different belief system. Some tell me they feel guilty about their feelings or questioning God. Don't. Whatever you feel is between you and your God. Y'all can work it out in time.

• • •

CHAPTER 4

Shock, Denial, Xanax, and Prozac

It was three months after Phil's death. The shock had worn off and I was hit with the reality of my loss. I'd called author and consultant Sam Horn, who is a friend and mentor, to give her an update.

About six months before Phil died, when he was in the hospital, I'd run into Sam at a networking luncheon. She knew about his illness and asked if I was writing about it. I told her that I was journaling and that maybe I'd write a book on caregiving.

"That's been done," Sam said. "What people really need to know is how you do this. Not one of the business women here today would suspect that you got dressed in your husband's hospital room and are going back to his bedside after this luncheon. How do you do it?"

That day was one of those "Wonder-Woman-I-can-do-anything" days. Do you ever have those? It's like when you're running a race, hiking a mountain, or preparing for a dinner party while juggling a major work assignment and you don't even flinch when the tray of wine glasses hits the floor. Adrenaline-fueled, totally focused, ready to conquer the world drive.

All my life I've lived in sprints. Taking on too much, running wide open, getting stuff done, and then coming to a dead stop. Sprint and rest. Sprint and rest. Put out a ton of work then lie on the couch for a couple days. I'd always wished I was one of those even-keeled, consistent people who have the Energizer bunny energy that goes on and on and on. I'm not. I'm more like a wind-up toy. A crisis or new idea gets me going at a frantic pace then I'm done. Rest, rejuvenate, restore until the next big thing.

Phil's illness had kept me in a constant state of crisis from the time of diagnosis. Many days were difficult and many nights I cried myself to sleep, terrified, anxious, and exhausted.

The day I ran into Sam I was Wonder Woman. I could write a book, take care of my husband, cure cancer, and leap tall buildings. When I called her months after he died the shock had worn off and some days even getting dressed seemed a gargantuan task. I wasn't sure I could handle simple tasks like paying bills, washing clothes, and putting on makeup. Let alone write a book on anything. And I had nothing to say. I didn't have any wisdom or answers. I only had sadness and questions that would never be answered.

Shock

"You've really been in a prolonged state of shock for eighteen months," my therapist, Robin, told me. "It started when he was diagnosed and has helped you function until now."

I usually think of shock as something that happens suddenly, like at a horrific accident where someone becomes confused or irrational. Robin explained that the type of shock I experienced when Phil was diagnosed made me become hyper-alert and sensitive to the situation. During the eighteen months of Phil's illness and treatment I seemed to be more focused and thinking more clearly than usual.

About nine months after his diagnosis, Phil was doing well and living life pretty much as usual. Well—our new usual—was working around his treatments and fatigue. I served on the board of a non-profit foundation and we were planning a big party for the founder's birthday. Phil and I agreed that since he was doing so well we'd host it at our house. A couple weeks before the date of the event he had another MRI and found that the tumor was growing. We needed to make another trip to the cancer center at Duke since they were directing his treatment.

The trip to Duke was the week before the event. We didn't know what we'd face there or how long we'd have to stay. The invitations for the event had already gone out. Before leaving for the appointment at Duke—a six-hour-drive each way—I had the house cleaned and pulled out all the wine glasses, dishes, preparation tools, and party supplies to get ready for the event. I gave another committee member a detailed list as to what food had been ordered and who was bringing what and where things were in my house. I left to take Phil to Duke with the instructions that if we needed to stay I'd call and let her know how to gain access to our house so she and the committee could come in and host the party without me.

Although the news at Duke wasn't good we came home the day before the party. I went into host mode while Phil slept and we hosted a party for about fifty people the next day. Phil rested in the bedroom until the start of the event then charmed everyone by tending bar as though nothing was wrong.

Looking back it seems totally crazy that we'd take that on. It would have been understandable to move the location of the party and notify the attendees.

Shock gave me the clarity of mind to outline the steps of what needed to be done, not just in this situation but throughout his illness. It also gave me the superhero focus that kept me from realizing I was doing entirely too much, some of which was unnecessary under the circumstances.

Shock can also make you feel numb, detached, and disassociated. This defense mechanism helps you handle situations that otherwise would bring you to your knees.

Like the day of Phil's seizure.

He had just come home from Florida where he went to Braves Spring Training with friends Ted and Ron. When they came home he seemed tired and disoriented. He went to take a nap and they went downstairs to the bar and called another friend, Bob, to join them.

When Phil awoke he pointed toward the clock and said a completely unintelligible sentence. We looked at each other, eyes wide open. This was bad news. I called Ted to come from the basement to sit beside Phil while I called the brain tumor clinic. The doctor instructed us to get him to the hospital immediately.

Ted was going to drive us to the hospital in his car while Ron drove our car there so we (or I) would have a way home. I put Phil in the backseat of Ted's car and buckled the seat belt. Just as I slid in from the other side, he started convulsing. I knew it was a severe seizure although I'd never seen one this severe before. I held him, telling him in a calm and in-charge voice that he was having a seizure and would be okay while at the same time shouting to Ted to call 911, what to tell them, and where to find the medications and information they'd likely need.

I was completely calm and unemotional throughout his seizure, the ambulance arriving, and answering the questions from the EMTs as they loaded him in the ambulance. Riding with them on the way to the hospital, I called both our mothers to let them know what had happened.

Later the guys told friends that I was like a rock. Strong and solid, seeming to know exactly what to do. Shock gave me uncommon clarity. Instead of getting hysterical I went into calm, control.

Sometimes increased physical strength is present, too. I'm sure you've heard of situations where someone lifted a car or carried a person to safety, exhibiting strength they normally wouldn't have.

When Phil was about to be released from the hospital after having the severe seizures I was worried. He had aphasia so he couldn't understand words spoken to him. He also didn't understand that he wasn't physically able to stand or walk. If he needed to go to the bathroom he'd just start getting out of bed. He didn't comprehend that he would fall when he tried to stand. In the hospital we'd had someone with him round the clock. They could call a nurse when he started getting up and make sure he didn't fall until she got there. At home it would just be me. I worried about him trying to get up while I was asleep beside him and falling before I awoke to help him into his wheel chair. I decided to turn our bed around so that one side would be against the wall. If he slept on that side he'd have to crawl over me to get up and that would wake me.

Excited to have found a solution, I got out of bed to move it into position before going to the hospital the next day. Our king-sized bed was huge. It was wooden with a large headboard and footboard. Very heavy. I couldn't move it alone. Especially with the box spring and mattress on it. So I tore an old towel into pieces. At the corner of the headboard I bent down, lifted the leg of the bed about half an inch off the floor with one hand, and stuck a piece of the towel underneath with the other. I did that for each leg so that there were towel pieces under each leg of the bed. The towel pieces could slide on the hardwood floor so I could slide the bed around into position. It was hard and I had to use all my strength to slowly, deliberately move the bed into position. A little distance at a time.

A couple weeks later, after Phil was home and the time came to get a hospital bed for him, I asked a couple guys to move the bed back into place. I'd tried and couldn't budge even one leg an inch off the floor. Mike Hood and Randy Foster were family friends but also building contractors who had built the screened porch onto the house and an authentic Irish pub in our basement. They moved and built things for a living. After getting the bed back to its usual place, Mike asked how I'd moved it before. I explained putting the towel pieces under each leg and sliding it around.

"We did the same thing," he said. Then he explained that it took both of them to move it and it was very heavy and difficult.

"I guess I had some adrenaline going," I shrugged.

"You must have," he nodded in disbelief.

That's the closest I came to having super-natural physical strength.

While shock can allow you to handle a crisis, even a prolonged one, it is a coping mechanism. People often cope well during the crisis but get sick afterward. Some even develop a type of Post-Traumatic Stress Disorder. After Phil's death I often had flashbacks of him in the hospital bed near death or of me bathing him or giving him medicine.

My sister said I was like a general when Phil died, giving everyone their orders. When he took his last breath I called hospice and told someone else to call the funeral home. As soon as hospice was finished with the necessary paperwork I gave my cell phone to one person and Phil's cell phone to another. I made two lists of people to call according to which phone would have the numbers. I then instructed them to make the calls telling family and friends that he had passed and the name of the funeral home to check for details.

One of the first calls was to Mini-Maids. I knew the house would be full of people for the next few days and wanted it to be clean. That's the type of clear, detached, goal-oriented thinking that shock can provide. Now I look back and laugh that I had someone call Mini-Maids before we even made the funeral arrangements. Like our family and friends would care if the house was clean.

Cynthia also reminded me that I was insistent that the hospital bed be removed and the bedroom furniture back in place immediately after Phil died. I knew his family was driving down from Tennessee for the funeral and I didn't want them to see it. I knew the sight of a hospital bed where Phil had spent his last hours would be sad for his mother and I wanted to save her from that pain. Like that little bitty detail would actually matter in the death of her son. I also had Mike and Randy tear down the wheel chair ramp they'd built into the garage only weeks before.

I couldn't bring back my husband or deal with his death but I could run a house. I guess it gave me somewhere to focus my energy and anxiety while I held on for a few more days to get through the funeral and burial. I thought I was mentally clear and strong but I look back now and see some crazy widow moments! But I'm grateful that the gift of shock gave me the mental clarity and strength to get through what I was going through.

Denial

The Merriam-Webster dictionary gives one definition of denial as "a psychological defense mechanism in which confrontation with a personal problem or with reality is avoided by denying the existence of the problem or reality."

We sometimes say someone is in denial and mean they just can't see the reality. We may even think they are stupid or irresponsible for not being able to see what's really happening. Sometimes it's just a way of coping so you can focus on what'll get you through to the next step. I found that denial can show up in many ways.

When Phil was diagnosed with a Stage IV Glioblastomia the prognosis was death in twelve to eighteen months. We didn't deny the diagnosis of the tumor. We just didn't accept the prognosis of impending death. We chose to believe that medical miracles happen and doctors/researchers are making new discoveries every day. Movies and books talk of "suspending your belief" so you can enjoy an unrealistic car chase or improbable event or a happy ending. Sometimes suspending your belief is a way to get through to the next phase.

We chose hope. Some people say that's false hope. I don't believe there is any such thing. There is hope and there is no hope. Hope gave us the strength to fight. The ability to focus on possibilities, not prognosis. Some may say that's denial but here's what I learned: I'd rather die with hope than live without it.

When it became obvious that his time on earth was winding down and he was no longer living with a brain tumor but losing ground to it every day, I would tell myself, "He may be dying but it won't be today." That may be denial but it gave me strength to take one day at a time.

Throughout his illness I closed my mind to the toll it was taking on my own body and mind. Like the day I ran into Sam Horn and felt like Wonder Woman. That's a type of denial too. I could have told you intellectually that my husband was near death and that I would likely get back to my writing and speaking business afterward. But I could not grasp the toll it was taking on me mentally and physically or understand how the whole experience would change me.

Once Phil was gone I never argued that he hadn't died. That would have been foolish. But knowing something in your mind and accepting it in your heart are two different things.

The bestselling memoir *A Year of Magical Thinking* written by author Joan Didion after the sudden death of her husband, talks about keeping everything at home the same as if he (her husband) was going to walk back in the door any minute. Another author spoke of sitting in the closet talking to her husband's clothes. I found myself going through Phil's clothes and re-arranging them, feeling close to him through them.

Recently I had lunch with an acquaintance who had lost her husband last year. She said, "I keep thinking he's going to walk back through the door."

None of us would deny that our husband or wife is dead. That he or she is never coming back. Yet sometimes we can't get our heads around how drastically our lives have changed. It takes a while, months I think, to get past the denial of our hearts and to come to terms with the hard, cold fact that the one we loved most is gone. Forever. And that our own lives have drastically changed because of it.

The gift of denial is that it allows you to focus on today.

Xanax and Prozac

"Tell me the exact words the doctor said that has you so upset."

My cousin, Melany, had called. She spoke briefly with Phil before talking to me. With my first words to her I started sobbing so hard that I couldn't even talk. She knew that we'd met with the doctor to find out the severity of Phil's brain tumor. It was stage IV. I'd been crying since we got the news. Although Phil and I had agreed not to tell our families the prognosis I blurted it out.

"He said Phil has only twelve to eighteen months to live," I sobbed.

"Oh. My. God. Myra." With hardly a breath, Melany continued in a calm, authoritative voice. "You have got to pull yourself together. Whatever time he has left you cannot spend it like this," she continued. "You have to be able to be strong and support him."

My next call was to my doctor. He prescribed Xanax and Prozac. Prozac was not new to me. I'd been on and off antidepressants for most of my adult life. I hadn't faced any trauma like this but I, like many people, have bouts of clinical depression. This is caused by the brain not producing enough of certain mood-regulating chemicals which leaves you feeling sad and depressed.

Once I got the medications in my system I was able to function normally. "I don't want to use a crutch," I often hear people say when someone suggests that they might benefit from antidepressants. Yet if you broke your leg severely and dragged yourself around on the floor or hopped from place to place people would think you were nuts. They'd tell you to use crutches or a cane and get on with life until your leg healed and you were able to get around normally.

Most of the widows and widowers I talk with seem embarrassed and apologetic to admit that they are on antidepressants. Yeah! You and half of America! If your body wasn't producing enough insulin or thyroid hormone no one would bat an eyelash at you for taking the meds to keep that in balance.

When you are going through prolonged trauma like caring for your husband or wife while they have a terminal illness, or if you've had the trauma of having someone die suddenly, it's perfectly alright to talk with your doctor about whether medications can help you. With antidepressants addiction isn't really an issue as they are designed for daily use. Take what you need to help you function as best you can and get on with your life!

Xanax is different. It's an anti-anxiety medication. It is possible to become addicted to Xanax and other drugs of that type so you'll want to use it wisely under a doctor's care. It can really take the edge off when you have a difficult day. When I went to the funeral home to make arrangements—the days of the visitation and funeral—the first time I saw the headstone I was very glad to have Xanax in addition to the antidepressant.

"I want to feel my feelings," is another excuse I hear people give for not taking mood-altering drugs. I guess if you're over-medicated maybe you don't feel your feelings. In my years of experience with antidepressants I've always had feelings. I laugh. I cry. I feel sad. I feel happy. I feel hurt. I feel disappointment. I feel embarrassed.

The key is that I feel the appropriate feeling for the situation. And to a manageable degree. After going on Prozac and Xanax for the bad days I didn't lose the ability to function. Yes, I still cried and grieved but I was not incapacitated by my feelings. I was able to function. Able to care for my husband until he died. Able to perform the minimum functions of my life in the early days of deep grief. Able to put one foot in front of the other and take baby steps forward until I was stronger. I did what worked for me without apology.

Putting It All Together

Phil's death was a trauma and I alternated between shock and denial. Over time I learned to give myself a break. I found that it takes time to create a new normal and things like a healthy diet, exercise, therapy, grief groups, massages, prayer, meditation, pajama days help heal your mind and body. "Normal" isn't the norm under these circumstances and I learned that the best I could do on any given day was enough. Looking back there were days when I was just a little crazy and days in which joy started to peak out from under the cover of sadness. And then there is the day I headed for bed and realized I had an entire day of joy.

• • •

41

I'd rather die with hope
than to live without it.

Myra McElhaney

CHAPTER 5

Don't Cry in the Liquor Store

"Are you finding everything you need?" the saleswoman asked with a helpful gesture and a smile.

I burst into tears at her innocent question. "My husband died," I sobbed, surprised at my own outburst. "He always bought the wine and I don't know what to get."

"Oh, let me give you a hug." She put her arms around me and said how sorry she was for my loss then offered to help me choose wine. Four hundred dollars later I had restocked my bar!

Yes, I think I got crying in public down to a fine art in those days. Even with Prozac and Xanax my eyes leaked a little sometimes when talking to someone about Phil's passing.

The key to crying in public is not to wipe your eyes. Just let the tears roll down your cheeks and then wipe them from your chin. This keeps your mascara from smearing around the eyes and making you look like a relative of Rocky the Raccoon. Waterproof mascara? I find it slides off my lashes, burns my eyes and can't be removed from my skin without makeup remover. Burning raccoon eyes that soap and water can't remove? I'll pass.

If you find that you're going into the ugly cry just mutter something about grieving and excuse yourself to the lady's room until you can pull it together. I promise you, they'll be glad you did! Very few people are able to handle a sobbing woman in a public place.

Jeannie Robertson, a friend and Southern humorist, has a funny bit in one of her speeches and YouTube clips about how people always react when they hear someone has died. In the South, at least.

"Oh, I'm so sorry," they'll say in a familiar sympathetic tone. Then they slightly bow their head and shake it a tad as if in disbelief. Sometimes I halfway expect them to cross themselves and say, "God rest his soul!" This reaction seemed customary when Phil had first passed away but since it's been a few years it feels a little weird. Now that I'm trying to date (Yes, trying. Dear God! More on that later.), when I meet guys or even talk to them by phone they'll do it. If I just move on with my sentence and don't acknowledge them they'll do it again, reach over to touch my arm, look me in the eye, and make sure I heard them, and say, "I'm so sorry for your loss."

Even now. It's been several years since I lost Phil but when someone asks if I'm married or somehow the subject comes up and I say that my husband died or that I'm widowed they do it just like Jeannie says.

"Thank you," I said to one guy. "I'm sorry for your divorce too."

"But that's not the same," he argued.

"Divorce is a loss too," I added.

"Yes, but it's not the same," he maintained. Like he'd know. He hadn't done a side-by-side comparison to the best of my knowledge. I let it go. No need to argue that I was just checking a box in this particular conversation. Married. Single. Separated. Divorced. Widowed. Boxes to check so people can categorize you accurately. Of course, being widowed is more than checking a box just as being married was more than checking a box in my life BPD (before Phil's death), but sometimes you just want to go on with the sentence or story and not have your marital status derail the conversation.

And while we're on the subject, widowed and divorced are not the same things. Many widows and widowers I know get a little testy about that. Some insensitive folks will say, "I know how you feel," and they'll say that their divorce was a loss too or that their grandma died or that they had to put down dear sweet Fluffy. No. It's not the same. Just so you know this is a very touchy point with us widowed folk.

I've lost my Daddy. I've lost four grandparents. Although I haven't had pets as an adult I'll never forget the day I heard the yelp of my little puppy and knew that "Boots" had gone to doggy heaven. It's not the same as losing your spouse.

On the other hand, being widowed has given me more sensitivity to my divorced family and friends. My sister divorced two years before Phil died. She was distraught and inconsolable. I tried to be there for her, support her, and be caring, but truly I just didn't get it. I'd had breakups before and knew the feeling of heartbreak but you cannot feel another person's pain. And you cannot make it go away.

After Phil died here's one thing I did begin to see clearly. When someone dies at an early age like my husband did, people will put their arms around you. They'll say, "This is horrible!" "This should never happen." "You don't deserve this." "I'm so sorry." "What can I do to help you?" They'll bring you casseroles. They'll offer to mow your grass. They'll take you out to dinner. They'll surround you with love and compassion. They'll give you a pass for most any idiot thing you do, excusing it because you're grieving.

When you're divorced people say, "Yeah, everybody's been divorced, get over it." No one brings casseroles or mows your lawn.

Not long after Phil passed a friend introduced me to one of her friends who was recently divorced. She did the "I'm sorry for your loss" head-nod thing. I told her that I was sorry for hers too and explained my observation of the differences and how widows get much more love and support. Weeks later she told me that it was the nicest thing anyone had ever said to her.

Once a divorced woman was complaining about her "wasband" (the man who was her husband) and said that maybe she'd have been better off if he'd died instead. I joked, "So you loved him so much that you'd rather have watched him suffer and die a horrible death than to have him go on to find happiness with another woman?" We both laughed.

Loss is loss. But they are not the same. Losing my husband was the worst thing I've ever experienced. I'd give anything if I could have him back. At the same time I didn't have to live through having the love we shared turn to hate. I didn't have to listen to the man I loved tell me that I was fat, ugly, or not good enough. I never had to wonder why he wanted someone else instead of me. I never had to see our wonderful life of memories distorted by having the relationship turn ugly. I lost my husband and that was devastating. I still get to keep the love. I now realize that with my divorced friends there's an extra layer of hurt. Loss is loss but they aren't the same.

If a divorced woman went into the liquor store and burst into tears because she didn't know what wine to buy I wonder if she'd be helped into hundreds of dollars' worth of wine and whisky, too.

Loss is difficult. It can leave you feeling fragile and broken. Someday you may find yourself crying in the liquor store or some other public place. Hopefully there will be someone to offer comforting words (that don't cost you hundreds of dollars). It's OK to cry. This stuff ain't easy.

• • •

Strange Bedfellows

"Misery acquaints a man with strange bedfellows," Trinculo famously states in Shakespeare's *The Tempest*. It's sometimes surprising the people we connect with in times of crisis. I'm not saying that any of my friends are strange, but several are folks I wouldn't have connected with except for my personal tempest. And in some cases, they were facing a storm of their own.

Drinking Buddy, Mark

"Mike, why is Mark calling me?" I questioned one of Phil's racquetball friends about another one I didn't know well.

"He called again wanting to know if I need help with anything." Mike repeated what he'd told me earlier about Mark just being a nice guy who thought maybe I needed help with the yard work or something. Mike isn't one to share anyone's personal details, but when I pressed he reluctantly shared that Mark was going through a divorce and probably lonely. That I understood!

I returned his call. "Mark, its Myra. Want to meet for a beer?"

"Yes! When?"

"Now!"

"How about Taco Mac?" Mark replied. "I can be there in thirty minutes."

I headed for my car hoping that I'd recognize Mark when I saw him. We'd met a couple times before Phil died. We'd gone to a party at his house. He and his wife had come to a party at ours. Then they attended the funeral and came by the house afterward along with many other friends and relatives.

Always surrounded by other people, I'm pretty sure he and I had never had a conversation beyond a casual greeting. I couldn't have described him if you'd asked.

He was walking toward the door when I pulled up and I recognized him immediately. We took a seat at the bar where we stayed for hours. We talked about his divorce. We talked about Phil. Two lonely, heartbroken people glad to have someone who understood to share a beer.

A few friends asked if Mark and I were dating or romantically involved. We just never were. He's about ten years younger than I and we're very different. I call Mark my 'bro-friend.' He's a boy but not a boyfriend and I talk to him like I would a girlfriend.

Mark is smart. An architect and an artist with a sharp wit. A really good man with strong values. He drinks beer; I drink wine. He wears graphic tees, cargo shorts, and flip-flops. I have my acrylic nails touched up every two weeks and never leave the house without makeup and my hair styled. (Well, sort of styled. A friend says I spend a lot of time working on my hair to make it look like I just got out of bed!) He's calm and logical. I'm an expressive extrovert. He's very direct and admits he doesn't have much of a filter. I try not to offend anyone and have always worried a bit too much about what people think. I wasn't much of a beer drinker until I started hanging out with Mark. We met regularly at dive bars (his choice, of course) and drank cheap beer. I realized that I could drink more cheap beer without getting drunk. That much wine and I'd have been snockered.

We talked. We listened. We laughed. We encouraged each other. We compared dating stories. I advised him on his girlfriends. He was the person I called before and after my first date. He pushed me to try online dating and offered to follow me to the restaurant if I didn't feel safe meeting a strange man alone. I can only imagine how that would have worked out.

"We were like two people in a three-legged race," Mark said recently when we were talking about the early days of our friendship. "Just holding on to each other and limping along."

Now he's engaged and I like his girlfriend. They come to my parties. I go to his. We live in different parts of town and don't see each other as much but I know he'd be here in a heartbeat if I needed him.

We first started hanging out because we were both lonely and felt broken. He quickly began to feel like a protective big brother, even though I'm older. I once told him that I thought if I was about to step in front of an oncoming train others might shout to warn me but he'd stop the train. He looked me in the eye and said with a nod, "I'd stop the train." I treasure my bro-friend, Mark.

Brain Tumor Widow Sister, Cynthia

About three months after Phil had been diagnosed with a GBM brain tumor I got an email from a woman named Cynthia. She told me that she was a friend of a friend and had heard about Phil's diagnosis. Her husband Vince had recently been diagnosed with the same thing and she wondered if we could talk. Of course! We exchanged phone numbers and planned a time for a call.

Coincidentally, not only are she and my sister both named "Cynthia" but her maiden name is the same as mine so she grew up with the same first and last name as my birth sister. Interesting, huh?

Cynthia lives in Asheville almost four hours away so we didn't get together but we talked every week or so throughout the illness of each of our husbands. They had the same diagnosis, the same surgery, and the same doctors at The Preston Robert Tisch Brain Tumor Center at Duke University. We compared notes about their treatments and talked about our feelings. We encouraged each other on difficult days and celebrated the good ones. It was comforting to have someone who understood so well what I was going through. It wasn't until both our husbands had passed almost two years later that we met in person.

Cynthia's birthday was coming up and she heard that jazz guitarist Pat Metheny was going to be in Atlanta. She and Vince loved his music and had seen him in concert before. Since Pat Metheny was appearing in the area only days away from the first birthday she would celebrate after losing her husband, Cynthia said that seeing him would be a fitting way to celebrate. (We widows are always looking for signs.) I'd never heard of Pat Metheny but was happy to go along and help celebrate her birthday.

Cynthia majored in horticulture in college and has a working farm where she raises asparagus. She also has chickens and honey bees. She grew up in South Georgia and went to college at UGA before developing a successful landscaping business in Savannah. After marrying and having a child, she and Vince decided they wanted to raise their son in a more rural environment so they moved just north of Asheville where Vince had a contracting business and she was a farmer. Quite a contrast from my life in the suburbs of Atlanta.

Phil had been in telecommunications sales. I had a speaking/writing business and we didn't have children. Although I grew up in rural North Georgia, the closest I'd gotten to farming in recent years was picking out vegetables at Whole Foods or buying "vine ripened" tomatoes at a roadside stand.

Cynthia is tall and slim with very short naturally grey hair and wears little makeup. What another friend refers to as a "naturallie" sort of gal. I'm a short redhead and let's say "curvy." Having been a makeup artist in the eighties I'm still fond of a painted face, acrylic nails, big jewelry, and bright colors. Plus black, of course. Lots of black and animal print in my wardrobe. I wondered if we'd have anything in common other than having shared a profound traumatic experience.

She arrived at my house between four and five in the afternoon. I remember that because I was watching Oprah. Cynthia may have thought I was a bit inhospitable since, rather than turning off the TV, I invited her in to watch the rest of the show. You see, Oprah time was sacred at my house. It was the time of day when I came out of my office and took a break. My target audience for speaking/writing is women and *The Oprah Winfrey Show* definitely kept its finger on the pulse of American women. I considered watching Oprah to be research. The nonfiction authors alone were worth watching the show for. Many trends I see today are things I first learned about on her show. I have been accused of drinking the Kool-Aid but I could do a whole book on how Oprah has influenced and shaped the interests of women in America. Anyway, it gave us time to give each other the once over and have something outside ourselves to discuss.

It's odd how, after knowing someone by phone for so long, I was a bit anxious at meeting in person. And especially since that first meeting was a whole weekend at my house. Would we actually like each other? Would we have anything in common other than being brain-tumor-widow-sisters?

We went to dinner before the concert and found we shared a love of good food and wine. That's always a good start. The concert was very entertaining and introduced me to a new and unique artist. We spent lots of time talking about our shared experience, our life before the whole brain tumor thing, and our hopes and fears. She's smart, always positive, and has a wicked sense of humor. We also have similar philosophies and outlooks on life. She blends in easily with a wide variety of people too. That's one of my favorite qualities in a person. I was able to see that in action since I'd overscheduled the weekend, as I often do.

My sister (the other Cynthia) was living with me at the time. While brain-tumor-widow-sister-Cynthia and I went to dinner and the concert, another long-time friend, June, arrived from Phoenix to spend the week. In addition to that, I was co-hosting a Pampered Chef party on Sunday afternoon at my house with another friend Gayle and we had about twenty guests to prepare for. Did I mention overscheduled?

We had "happy chaos" that weekend, as there often is in my life. Sister-Cynthia, BTWS-Cynthia, June, and I worked together on Saturday prepping foods for the party. On Sunday, Gayle and her sister, Brenda joined the fun and we set everything up, put out the foods and prepared to meet our guests. The Pampered Chef consultants arrived early. One was experienced. The other was a friend-of-a-friend so Gayle and I had agreed to co-host her first party. With twenty guests and the Mimosas flowing we had lots of fun and her sales were impressive. I don't think even the experienced consultant had sold as much in one party!

BTWS-Cynthia and I got to know each other better and have remained friends, talking regularly by phone and visiting each other a few times a year. Sometimes I hear women say they are not interested in widow/widower groups as they don't have any interest in meeting someone with whom the only thing they have in common is having been widowed. I do understand that but I believe that when we take the time to get to know someone we usually find that we have more things in common than we expect. There are some things only someone who has traveled the same road can understand. Having Cynthia as my brain-tumor-widow-sister has certainly eased the road a bit for me. I'm very thankful for her friendship. And gifts of fresh asparagus.

New friends help us to move forward. Over the years our friendship has grown and we don't talk much about our dead husbands. We just share what's happening in our lives and encourage each other in new adventures. Her philosophy is, "Double down on the fun!"

This year she took an exciting six-week cross-country driving trip and invited several friends to join her for segments. I traveled with her for eleven days, from Seattle to Denver. We got along easily. She cheerfully went along when I had to visit a nail salon the first day I was there. I'd broken a nail and you know you can't go camping with a broken nail! She got a pedicure and camping we went.

She brought along all the equipment and I was ready to say "Yes!" to adventure. Setting up tents at night and making coffee on the gas stovetop in the morning came back to me easily although I hadn't camped in many years. We mixed up the trip with camping and hotel stays. We visited some of her friends, visited some of my friends, ate at fancy restaurants, and had roadside picnics. We visited big cities, small towns, Yellowstone Park, national forests, canyons, and hot springs. We saw wildlife, amazing views, and met interesting people. I think traveling through the fields of Idaho would have been boring with anyone else. Her horticulture background provided a wealth of information about what crops we were passing and the irrigation techniques. Without her narrative it would have all looked like green fields to me. People we met assumed we were life-long friends. No one would have guessed that we were just two crazy widows ready to double down on fun!

Friends who have shared our experiences and share our attitude about moving forward in life are a special gift.

Looking at my life now, there are many people I wouldn't have met in my BPDD (Before Phil's diagnosis/death) life. I would give anything to have Phil alive and to be living the life we had planned together. But that's not an option. Filling my life with bright, fun, fascinating people still is.

• • •

CHAPTER 7

Layers of Loss

On the TV drama *Grey's Anatomy*, best friends Meredith Grey and Christina Yang have popularized the term your "person." It defines that one person in your life that always has your back. Your "person" is the first one you want to call to share good news and the one you know will hold you when there's bad news. The one you share everything with. The one who'll always be there for you and you for him/her. For most of us, when we lose our spouse we lose our "person."

There are so many layers to losing your "person." You lose the relationship, the traditions, the routines, the plans, and the dreams. The person you share so many memories with. The one you've planned your future with.

For couples with kids you lose the other parent. Some widows and widowers lose their financial security when the primary breadwinner dies or by going from two incomes to one. Some lose their homes. Some lose family members when there is conflict between in-laws or siblings.

You lose your marital status, which is so much more than just checking a different box when you fill out a form. I always feel sort of lost when a form asks to list an emergency contact person. Sometimes I just want to write, "In case of emergency call 911." It's quite an adjustment to start living your life as single rather than half of a couple. So many "we" decisions now are "me" decisions. I miss having a partner to discuss major decisions. I miss having my "person" to tell about my day or to ask for advice.

Getting rid of their clothes and things, trading "their" car, selling "our" house—each time you give up something that was part of your life together it feels like another little layer of loss.

A big loss for many widows and widowers is the loss of friends. Your social network changes. Sometimes dramatically. It's always a surprise to see who steps up and who stands back.

Was My Invitation Lost in the Mail?

"I'm sorry. I just didn't think about inviting you," a friend apologized for not including me when a few other couples had gotten together for dinner. His apology clearly defined the problem.

The friend didn't even think about inviting me. Now that I wasn't half of a couple I just wasn't thought of. I'd become a party of one without the party. I'd heard from other widowed and divorced people that your friends will stop calling. I didn't think it would happen to me.

Our friends were amazing in the way they surrounded us throughout Phil's illness. While he was still feeling well enough to live life as usual, they traveled with us and went out with us, always acting as though nothing was wrong. Just what Phil wanted and needed. They made a lot more time to be with him. Soaking up as much "Phil time" as they could and letting him know with their presence how important he was to them. When he was too sick to get out they brought food, helped with household chores like mowing grass and running errands, sat with him in the hospital, and helped me in whatever way they could. I could not have gotten through the illness and death without our friends.

New Year's Eve was always a big deal for us. Phil hosted the annual New Year's Eve party for his friends even before we met. When we dated and got married we continued the tradition through the end of the millennium. In 1999 we decided to take a break and start celebrating New Year's Eve in other ways so we threw one big final New Year's Eve party to, as the Prince song says, "Party like it's nineteen-ninety-nine." Then we switched to hosting Christmas parties and traveling or getting together with smaller groups of friends to ring in the New Year.

In the fall 2007, Phil commented that he didn't want to host a Christmas party that year. I thought that odd, given how he loved parties and was always the one to initiate them. I agreed without even asking why. Looking back, had we had a party it would most likely have been scheduled for the very week he was diagnosed with the brain tumor. Strange coincidence, huh?

When Phil was diagnosed in December of 2007, we again hosted our close friends, the "inner circle" as I called them, for those last two New Year's eves.

The first New Year's Eve after Phil's death, one of the couples in the inner circle hosted a NYE party at their house so I was there with a few of our friends. That's the last New Year's Eve I've been with any of them.

Okay, New Year's Eve is kind of a big deal and not that many people want to host parties. Everyone has their own preference of how they like to ring in the New Year. I get that.

In addition to NYE or Christmas, ours was usually the party house. We often had what I call impromptu parties. Phil would say something like, "I'm going to grill tenderloin. I think I'll call Ted and see if he can come." Then he'd report back that Ted was in, and so was Gary, and Larry and Susan, and he'd suggest that I call a few of my friends. Next thing you know there were ten people coming for dinner when the day before we didn't even have any plans.

Other times he'd pick a restaurant and start making calls. There would be six or eight of us gathering for dinner somewhere. In addition to that there would often be dinner with one or two other couples.

Phil loved parties and was sort of the ringleader for our group of friends. Somehow I thought that the group would still get together after he was gone, only now it would be up to me to keep it going. A few times during the year after Phil's death I threw parties as "we" used to do. I invited the same people. Some came. Some didn't. I never said anything but it always hurt my feelings when they didn't come. A few of the folks I've never seen again since he died. Several others I've seen a few times but they never came to another party at our house.

One of the other couples in our group had a few parties the first couple years too. Whether at my house or theirs, talk always came back to Phil. We'd end up sharing memories and "Phil stories."

On the one-year anniversary of his death I threw a party. Not to celebrate his death but so we could be together with our memories of him.

It was a small group. Just nine of us around the table sharing memories of Phil.

I came to realize that hosting the parties was just too painful. I was trying so hard to keep the gang together but it wasn't the same and I usually ended up feeling sadder that he wasn't there. I think our friends did too.

Family of Friends

Fortunately, we had lots of friends. We had "his" friends, "our" friends, and "my" friends. There were some surprises with people who backed away and others who stepped up.

One big surprise was Phil's guy friends who stepped up to watch over me. His best friend Ted has become one of my closest friends and advisors. Phil had said to look to Ted for help with understanding the investments and he's become someone I discuss major decisions with and go to for advice.

Gary, another of Phil's friends, was getting a divorce when Phil died. He stepped in to watch over me and Pat, a neighbor of his who had also recently divorced. Once when Phil was sick, Gary called to say that he was coming to sit with Phil and had made an appointment for me and Pat at a local nail salon for a manicure and pedicure. That was such a thoughtful gesture and wonderful gift. After Phil died he checked on me regularly and we often went to lunch or dinner. Soon he and Pat began dating. Sometimes the three of us go out. Occasionally Gary and I still meet for lunch or dinner to talk and catch up.

Mike, one of Phil's racquetball buddies, and his wife Vikki had become good friends that we traveled with and had dinner with often. After Phil died Mike sent a text almost every day just to check in. The texts tapered off gradually but he's never missed sending a message on Phil's birthday or the anniversary of his death. They invite me over for dinner and to go to events and still invite me to travel with them. I've never had the sense of being a third wheel with them. They've become some of my closest and dearest friends.

It's Not You, It's Me

If you watched the TV show *Seinfeld*, you probably think of George Costanza when you hear the "it's not you, it's me" routine. We've all heard it as an easy way to break up with someone by letting them down gently. Sometimes it's true that we are the one that changes.

It seems after Phil died that I became very sensitive to the energy of people around me. I think that's common after physical or emotional trauma. Because of this I don't enjoy the company of some friends I used to like being around.

I've always had a lot of girlfriends, especially through business, who are "A-type" drivers with high energy and focused on achievement. Always doing. Sometimes with an almost hyper-active energy. I now find that type of energy difficult to be around for long periods of time. I also find it difficult to be around negative people who are always critical and complaining.

My own energy and focus has changed over the past few years and this means that I need more time alone and have to be more sensitive to my own energy. I need to be careful in choosing how I spend my time and energy.

Overall, I'm richly blessed with friends. There's an old saying that some people are in our lives for a lifetime, some for a reason and some for a season. One thing I've learned is to value and enjoy friendship and be willing to let go.

To Ski or Not to Ski

Phil, Ted, and Ron had started skiing together back in their twenties, before Phil and I met. Over the years the group changed with people coming and going but for the past several years there was a core group of about six couples, including Phil and me. Some went every year, others now and then. Ron's girlfriend Rhonda went whenever work permitted. Ted took a girlfriend now and then. So there was often a single making it an odd number. The year after Phil was diagnosed there were eleven of us in Jackson Hole. The next year, Phil defied doctor's orders and went snow skiing anyway. Seven of us went to Vail. None of us went skiing the winter after Phil died.

One of the couples I have not seen since Phil died, except for accidentally running into them in the grocery store once. Another I've seen a few times over the years. One couple decided to ski with their adult children for an annual family trip. Rhonda hasn't been able to go the past few years because of work. Ted and Ron decided to make skiing a guy's trip and invited a couple of their male friends.

I wanted to keep skiing but didn't for several years. I love skiing although I'm not great at it. Usually I ski a solid green slope (easiest) and sometimes can do blue (intermediate). I guess that makes me a turquoise skier. Black is advanced. I did ski a blue/black slope once. I came back black and blue.

Finally, I talked a new friend, Susan Reece, into going with me. The first year we went alone. Next we went with the Atlanta Ski Club. I still miss "our group" and the way we did things but at least I didn't let losing Phil and the group splitting up stop me from something I enjoy. Skiing still brings back floods of memories and Susan is patient when I'm rattling on about recognizing places from the past and boring her with stories of past ski trips. Now another friend has joined us and we'll likely find others as we keep going.

Recently, when having coffee with another widow friend, talk turned to travel. She said she doesn't travel much anymore because she misses the way she and her husband traveled together. I do too. Losing the way we traveled together is another layer of the loss.

Oh, Those Lonely Weekends!

"I'll make it alright from Monday morning 'til Friday night. Oh, those lonely weekends!" These lyrics from an old song by Waylon Jennings came to mind a lot after Phil died.

Before marrying Phil, I worked for many years in the cosmetics industry, calling on retail stores in the southeast. Back in those days I worked on Saturdays, some Sundays and most holidays. Time off for me wasn't always weekends and I didn't have much of a social life. I might go out with friends but that was about it. Vacations were just occasions to catch up on projects or visit friends in other areas. I traveled some with work but not too much personally.

Phil thought every weekend was an occasion for a party and every holiday was a reason to take a trip. Vacations were a big deal. He taught me how to have fun! It was an easy lifestyle to get used to.

After Phil died, Friday nights and Sunday afternoons were the worst. Phil traveled for work so usually he came home Friday nights and the weekend started. We might go to dinner, have people over, or just go out for Mexican food and margaritas. Whatever the plan, it signaled the start of the weekend.

Sundays were usually just the two of us. Many Sundays we'd ride the motorcycle to brunch and take a long ride into the mountains. Afterward we'd make a huge bowl of popcorn or put on a pot of chili or beans on the stove to simmer for supper. Phil would watch golf or football on TV while I'd lie beside him and read. Sometimes we'd watch an old TV movie or take a nap. It was quiet, intimate time together when we would just enjoy being alone as a couple. Relaxing, cuddling, laughing, and dancing in the kitchen as we made dinner.

After Phil died I'd get anxious if I didn't have plans for Friday nights and holidays. Saturday nights at home weren't so bad as long as I had something to do on Friday nights. Sunday afternoons I could get out of the house for a convertible drive, a movie, or go shopping. If I didn't have anyone to go with I didn't mind doing those things alone. Sometimes a good book would get me through a Sunday afternoon.

ArtsCard and "The List"

About six months after Phil died I got together with a couple friends I knew through a business networking organization. One of them had a business called ArtsCard where you bought a membership that gave discounts for arts venues around Atlanta. She needed someone to write a newsletter and blog for her. She couldn't pay but could give free tickets to events. Theatre, opera, symphony, museums, the botanical gardens—so many things that I loved but didn't take time for since Phil and I lived in the suburbs and were usually hanging out with friends or out of town for weekends and holidays. This gave me an incentive to do these things and came at just the right time. I needed to be out building my own social life and free tickets gave me the "what" to do. Now I just had to find the "who" to go with me.

I did something that I've since advised many widows and widowers to do. I made a list of the single people I knew who might be available and interested to go to something with me. The list included names, phone numbers, and email addresses.

When I got tickets to an event I'd go down my list until I found someone who was available to share my free tickets and go with me. Usually we'd have dinner before the event. This gave both me and a friend a fun, cheap night out. Or maybe not so cheap, depending on where we went for dinner.

Not only did this entice me to see plays, movies, concerts, and museums that I never would have made the effort to see, it also helped me connect with many other single, divorced, and widowed friends that I might not have followed up with.

I've been involved with business networking groups for years and I meet lots of people. I've often said, "Let's get together sometime," but then I don't follow up. Having a free pair of tickets for a specific date motivated me to find someone to go with me. And that would give us a chance to talk and get to know each other better and have a shared experience. Sometimes what starts as an activity buddy grows into a deep friendship.

Free tickets also got me into unfamiliar neighborhoods. I had no idea that Atlanta had so many small community theaters and such great acting talent. Writing the newsletters and blogs got me back into writing too. It gave me a fun project to focus on that wasn't a full-time job and was flexible enough that I could work it around anything else I was doing.

I've never really enjoyed being an organizer. I'm not good with details and don't like planning events or coordinating groups of people. However, working with ArtsCard even got me to plan some small group events. Jennifer Langley, the ArtsCard founder, also has an event planning business. She planned annual ArtsCard events, inviting ArtsCard members, and I'd invite all the people on my list of single, divorced, and widowed friends. A few times I'd pick a play or concert, then send an email with the details to my "list," asking if they were interested. I'd buy tickets for the group and they'd pay me individually. It was fun to have a group to go with.

As things changed with ArtsCard and I was no longer working with them or getting free tickets, I still kept the list but I don't have to refer to it as much these days. Over the years several people on the list have become friends who also invite me to get together for dinner, drinks, or events. I've made new friends and new routines and get frequent social invitations. Occasionally I email about fundraising and networking events I'm involved with. I often get replies saying, "I can't make this one but keep me on the list!"

I learned that the best way to rebuild a social life is to make a list of names with numbers and emails. When I wanted to go someplace specific or just wanted someone to have dinner with I went down the list until someone said "Yes." Sometimes I spent time with people I otherwise wouldn't but mostly I made some very good friends from what had been just acquaintances. I reminded myself not to be discouraged if it took several calls to get a "yes." To paraphrase a classic Beatles song, "You'll get by with a little help from your single friends." Even if you have to find new ones.

Draw New Circles

There's an old poem by Edwin Markham that says, "He drew a circle that shut me out—Heretic, rebel, a thing to flout. But Love and I had the wit to win: we drew a circle and took him in!"

Many of us see that our circles change after we lose a spouse. Some friends stop calling. You may not feel anything in common with others anymore. Don't let yourself get isolated.

Medical News Today reports evidence that "the risk of developing and dying from heart disease can depend on the strength of one's social network of friends and family, and that being recently widowed can increase one's odds of dying."

Social engagement is very important to mental and physical health. When you're young, it's easy. You tend to be surrounded with people who are of similar age and life stage. College, young marrieds, couples with children, etc. Having children in school often gives a built-in social life as you're involved in sports, band, or theatre, and you meet other parents, even some single ones, at your children's activities.

As you get older and the kids are doing their own thing or have moved away it's easy to get into a rut of work, household chores, and nothing else. Even if you work out at a gym it isn't likely you'll make friends there unless you're participating in a team sport. Some people meet others in church but often I hear widows say that all their church friends are couples.

We don't like thinking that social life takes work but sometimes it does. An article in *Psychology Today* says we currently have an "epidemic of loneliness" and since humans are social creatures, that presents some emotional and physical problems.

Making a list and calling several people until you get a "yes" may sound like work. If you do it for a while you'll likely get to the point of not needing the list because you've developed a new social network. It's well worth the effort.

Yes, it hurts when people we've known stop calling. If you really want them to stay in your life, keep calling them. Draw a new circle that brings them in. Maybe they need a little time to get over losing their friend too. Maybe they move from being every weekend get-together friends to being once or twice a year friends, but don't give up if you love them.

You can make new circles of people who are also widowed, single, or divorced. You'll likely find more in common with them at this stage of your life. They may just start as "activity buddies" to share a play, a concert, or take in a festival. Close friendships build over time so keep asking, keep going, keep saying "Yes" and build new circles that draw in people you want in your new life. It's worth it!

• • •

CHAPTER 8

Condolences and Sympathy

"So how are you doing? I mean really?" a friend said, tilting her head to the side with a sad look of pity as she emphasized the "reeea-lly?"

I know she meant well but it seemed as if she truly wanted me to collapse into sobs and breakdown before we headed out to the lunch we'd planned. Like she wanted to be "the one" that I'd come unglued with. I was seeing my therapist regularly as I prefer to do my sobbing with a trained professional. I wanted my friends to distract me with getting out, going places, and telling me of their lives rather than talking about grief, loss, cancer, and death. Most were easily able to pick up clues as to how to be there for me. Others seemed to be watching for the big breakdown. I hated that.

"That's just not you," a neighbor said as I told her about the friend. I stood a little straighter. That's not me. I did cry in public and with several friends but it was the eyes filling with tears kind or a few tears rolling down my cheek. Not the sobbing, sniffling, "ugly cry" as Oprah calls it. My therapist said maybe I shouldn't try to be so strong but it's how I am. I was always the one people tell their problems to. Not the one needing comforting. I hate being pitied. I can't explain it but there's a different feel between being comforted and being pitied.

I know what it's like to try to console someone who is inconsolable. Someone who's sobbing and shaking. Once when I received a late night call from a friend whose husband had just asked for a divorce I was listening and slowly repeating, "Oh, honey!" "That's okay." "Let it out." "It's alright." "You're going to be okay." She cried it out and was able to calm down enough to tell me what was going on.

"I don't know how you do it," Phil said, overhearing the beginning of the call. I know to just listen, comfort, and not try to fix or offer suggestions until the emotion is calmed.

That's okay for a call or two but when someone goes into heaving sobs every time you see them you quickly begin to feel helpless and emotionally drained. I never want to do that to any of my friends. Besides, I'm so attached to being strong and resilient I wouldn't want to damage my image!

Corny Condolences

There isn't a handbook for what to say and what not to say to someone who's grieving. I wish there were. Every widow and widower I know has had someone say something to them that was not helpful. It's a topic that often comes up on a Facebook page for widows/widowers that I follow. Sometimes just telling our, "can you believe they said that?" story brings some relief. Having someone who's been there to say, "You're right, they just don't get it."

Things I Hated Hearing:

"What doesn't kill you makes you stronger."

Nice quote. There's even a song about it. Not helpful to the recently widowed. This quote is perfect for chemo. The poison they put in your body hoping it'll kill cancer cells before it kills you. It can make you so sick you think you're going to die but if the chemo and/or cancer doesn't kill you and you survive you'll get strong again. If it doesn't kill you it'll make you stronger.

"God doesn't give us more than we can handle."

Excuse me but I don't see God as some personal trainer in the sky that gives you as much weight as you can handle and when you survive that, then ups the ante to keep building your strength until you're a hulk. No, I think God will help you handle whatever you're given but I don't believe that God singles out the strong and gives them tragedy. Personally, I hate this quote. It reminds me of telling my (then) doctor that I couldn't believe Phil was diagnosed with a brain tumor only seven months after Daddy died. He said, "Maybe God gave you that as practice for handling this." Huh? You honestly believe that?

"Everything happens for a reason."

Really? My husband, who was a wonderful man, got a brain tumor and died and I'm supposed to think there's some reason that'll make that OK with me? I don't think so. I've always been a positive person and believed that all things work together for good. Like the Darius Rucker song, "This" he sings about how all the things that didn't work out and the many heartache and hard times he endured ". . . all lead me here to you." I used to believe that every bad relationship, every job opportunity that didn't work out, every plan that fell through was preparing me for something better. Until Phil died. I do not believe that I'll ever get to a place in my life where I'll look back and say, "Oh, yeah, this is worth losing Phil for!" Never.

"You're young you'll remarry."

Yeah, if I could just quit crying long enough to look for a replacement husband everything would be just hunky-dory!

"I know just how you feel."

I'm sorry but losing Grandma or having Fluffy put down just ain't the same thing.

"At least he's no longer suffering."

Right. He isn't suffering now. I am. Just shut up!

Just Admit that There's No Explanation

One day not long after Phil was diagnosed, I met with fellow author and speaker Tricia Molloy who is very spiritual. I was questioning how and why this came into our lives.

"So you want answers," Tricia said. That was it. No advice. No ideas as to why. Just a simple statement. Tricia, who had been widowed as a very young woman with two small children and was now happily married, didn't offer anything more. A testament to her wisdom. The statement stuck in my mind and eventually I came to be at peace with knowing that there are questions I'll never have answers to. In this lifetime, anyway.

I remember when

Most widows/widowers enjoy talking about the life of their loved one, not talking about the death. When Phil was sick and after he died I enjoyed having people contact me by phone, email, or messages on the CaringBridge.com website to tell me how they met or something specific they remembered about him. Even people that I didn't know who had worked with him or gone to school with him. I liked being reminded that he touched the lives of everyone he met and that he was fondly remembered.

With close friends I loved sharing stories or mentioning what Phil might say about this or that. It never made me sad. Talk of death and missing him did.

"I'm so sorry! I always make you cry," a close friend said one day at lunch.

"No, you let me cry. There's a big difference."

She is one of the inner circle friends and of course anytime we were together the first couple years after the funeral, talk quickly turned to Phil. Tears would well up in my eyes and I'd dab the corners or maybe one or two would roll down my cheek. I wasn't anywhere near a full-on cry. Just releasing sadness at missing him. Avoiding all talk of him would have been more painful and awkward than talking about him. His presence (and absence) was still so strong in our lives. Then conversation would quickly move on to other subjects and we'd enjoy lunch or dinner.

People really do want to help even though they may be clumsy in knowing how to express it. None of us is perfect and I know I've made some of these blunders myself. Even after my own loss.

A few years after Phil died a former client called. He wanted to get together so he could get my opinion on a business idea. I hadn't seen him since Phil's funeral. When I asked how his wife was doing he told me she had died the year before. Shocked, I blurted out, "Oh my God! What happened?"

"It's a long story, I'll tell you about it when we meet," he replied. I realized then that my stupefaction at suddenly learning that he'd lost the wife he adored was just as blundering as anything anyone had said to me in my loss.

Condolences and sympathy are awkward for most folks. Even if people say the wrong thing it's better than not showing up at all.

• • •

Being able to live well,
laugh again, and enjoy your
own life does not mean you
didn't love the one you lost.
It just means you are not
letting the tragedy in your
life claim you both.

Myra McElhaney

CHAPTER 9

Married to a Dead Person

Two years after my husband died, his mother lost her husband. A few days after his funeral she asked me to help her look over some paperwork from insurance companies, social security, and other stuff. I picked up a piece of paper requiring a signature stating that "the marriage ended in death."

The marriage ended in death. The words were a punch to the gut. I re-read them several times thinking of my own marriage. The marriage ended. Yes, I knew that my husband had died. I knew that we'd married "until death do us part." I knew that my legal marital status was no longer "married," it was now "widowed." Yet until that moment I did not fully and completely feel what it meant that my marriage had ended. Up until that moment I'd been married to a dead man. I had let go of him being around but I had not let go of our marriage.

I once read the memoir of a well-known woman who had lost her son. In talking about it she said that she had been his mother and that, since he was gone, she was mother to his memory. She talked about creating a memorial to him, about visiting the grave daily and talking to him and about doing things in remembrance of him to keep his memory alive. After seeing the words, " . . . the marriage ended in death" I realized that I'd been doing that too.

In the first year there is so much to do after the funeral—handling probate, changing names on accounts, transferring car titles, and other tasks that are about losing a husband. I was sort of like a trailing spouse. Often when corporate executives get transferred they move on to temporary housing at the new location to start the job. The spouse, usually the wife, stays back at the old house to get the kids through the end of the school year, ready the house to sell, oversee the sale of the house, and close accounts for utilities and other services. At the same time she's looking for a new house, preparing for new schools, and opening new accounts in the new location. And all this before moving day.

Handling the paperwork associated with someone dying and taking over all the stuff Phil had handled, like managing our investments and overseeing the lawn care and home maintenance, seemed like a full-time job. Without him there to guide me I had to figure out a lot of things on my own. There was a big learning curve. Still, it felt temporary. Like I was getting things ready to go be with him.

You often hear of couples, especially older couples, where one dies shortly after the other. When Dana Reeve, wife of actor Christopher Reeve, died in 2006 I remember thinking that she'd gone on to be with him. You'll recall, he became a quadriplegic after an accident in an equestrian competition. For nine years she was the face of love and strength beside him as he lobbied for causes related to spinal cord injuries and stem cell research. They started the Christopher Reeve Foundation and were involved in various projects bringing attention and funding to find new treatments for paralysis. She was diagnosed with lung cancer less than a year after he died and within eighteen months after he passed she was gone too.

I truly did think that I'd die a few years after Phil. Believing we were soul mates, I just couldn't see life without him and figured I'd follow him on to the other side quickly. My doctor must have been concerned about my health too. After my annual physical he sent me for various tests including a heart scan. Hundreds of dollars later, they discovered I was simply over-weight and middle-aged. Guess that won't kill you. At least not quickly.

Well, I Almost Died

About six months after Phil died I ended up in the emergency room but my sister saved my life. Twice.

She was living with me at the time and took me to my doctor with what seemed to be a sudden onset of flu-like symptoms. My doctor couldn't work me in and after one look recommended I go across the street to the emergency room. I was so weak that a nurse offered to take me in a wheelchair. In the ER they first thought it was flu but when tests showed it wasn't they began searching.

By this time my skin and eyes were beginning to look yellow, a sign of jaundice. Not good. They gave me Delaudid for my pain, which made me feel very happy. An ER doctor came to my bedside and said, "You are very sick. Very sick." He shook his head and explained that they didn't know the cause but would continue to run tests. I looked up at him cheerfully and said, "Okay!" He seemed to think that I didn't get the severity of the situation. Hey, I was a recent widow and I had Delaudid. I really didn't care!

Turns out there was a gall stone lodged in my bile duct. They had to do an endoscopic procedure inserting a stent into the duct so it could heal. But I don't have a gallbladder. I'd had it removed about five years earlier. Strangely enough, I'd had complications a few days after the surgery and required the same stent procedure then.

After a few days in the hospital, receiving large doses of antibiotics to cure the infection, I was sent home and scheduled to come back in a week or so to have the stent removed.

Surprise! The Atlanta area got a big snow and ice storm that week. Airports and schools were closed. For the first time I remember hospitals even cancelled all non-emergency surgery because doctors couldn't get to the hospitals. My procedure was rescheduled. No big deal, right? Wrong.

Between the time the ice melted and the day I was to go in for my re-scheduled procedure I began feeling very sick. I'd gone to lunch with a dear friend and she noticed I was looking pale during lunch. Knowing the situation, she offered to drive me to the hospital but I said I'd be okay. I wasn't. When Cynthia came home from work a few hours later she had to take me back to the emergency room. They admitted me, removed the stent, and kept me a few days because the stent had been in too long and had gotten infected.

When I went to the gastroenterologist a few weeks later for a follow up visit he didn't recognize me. That's how drastically different the sick me looked from the healthy me. Scary, huh?

Was That a Chance for Me to Go?

Some people believe that God, the heavens, the powers that be give us a few opportunities in life to choose to stay or to go. Maybe that's true, maybe not. I don't pretend to know how the universe operates. I do believe that Cynthia is the reason I didn't die. Not just because she took me to the ER. I didn't have much of a will to live but I could not die with her living in my house.

Now that may sound mean but had I died while she was living with me in that house it would have been harder on her than at any other time in her life. She would have been faced with quickly finding a new home, having to prepare my house for sale, having to dispose of all my worldly possessions, having to plan a funeral. And all this while she was still reeling from losing her brother-in-law and watching her only sister deal with grief. Not to mention being only a few years away from her divorce and the loss of our daddy.

Nope. I couldn't die yet. I still had things to take care of. Lots of things. Unconscious choice or just the way things happened? I don't know. Either way, I'm still here.

In Loving Memory

I've noticed that in the first year after losing a spouse, widows and widowers usually look for ways to memorialize the dearly departed. I think this is part of still feeling married to the dead spouse. We're trying to make something lasting that will honor their memory. Some plant trees or build monuments. Some start foundations or scholarship funds.

I'd served on the board of a non-profit foundation and knew that starting one was not something I wanted to do. Besides, there were several foundations already dedicated to brain tumor research. It would be more effective to support them rather than starting my own.

The McElhaney Pub Team

I decided that I'd honor Phil by raising money to support brain tumor research. I contacted my graphic designer, Vanessa Lowry, about creating a logo for the McElhaney Pub. I sat at the kitchen table looking up Irish type symbols on the computer to give her an idea of what I'd like. As I was thinking, I looked out the window and realized that the black wrought iron railing that Phil had designed for our porch was all scrollwork.

Commonly used in Irish symbols. I sent a photo to Vanessa and she used that as inspiration for the McElhaney Pub logo, combined with other shapes I liked. I wanted it to be green since that was Phil's favorite color and very Irish. She added yellow and a burnt orange. Without realizing it she'd picked "earth tones" that Phil wore often enough for his friends to tease him about it. I loved the logo she designed.

I ordered McElhaney Pub T-shirts with the logo to sell for brain tumor research. I was so excited when Phil's former employer ordered a couple hundred of them that I doubled the order! Our friends and family bought a few. I put together a team for the Southeastern Brain Tumor Foundation's annual Race for Research and the McElhaney Pub team wears the shirts every year.

Twice I've had people contact me about shirts because they had been researching the name "McElhaney" and found the pub's Facebook page. One guy was in England!

Change for Brains

Donating to one of Phil's favorite charities was another way I chose to honor his memory. I donated his change. He had a lot of change.

Phil had told me that when he was about ten years old he wanted a mini bike but his mother said they couldn't afford to buy one. Industrious as he was even at that young age, Phil "hired out" to local farmers to earn the money on his own. He saved his pay and had his mom take him to the bank to open a savings account. Upon opening the account, the bank gave him a "piggy bank" that looked like a robot. He quickly filled it with change. That was the start of his collection of change. No, not a coin collection—Phil saved his change. In banks. In jars. In dishes. Like many people he would empty his change into a container rather than carry it in his pockets. The jars and dishes of change began to grow.

When we married Phil had a five-gallon pickle jar about half full of change, in addition to a dish or mug here and there. I gave him a few piggy banks over the years and he would fill them with specific coins. Quarters in one, nickels in another, dimes in a different one. I joked with him about hearing of an old man who died and left jars of money all over his house. I said that I'd never understood why someone would have money in jars but after seeing Phil's change collection I could now understand. I kidded him that when he died he would also leave jars of money all around the house. Little did I know.

When Phil died and I was preparing to sell our house I found lots of change in unexpected places. While cleaning out his home office I saw two large popcorn tins on a bottom shelf and thought, "Now, why would he keep those?" and I went to throw them away. I couldn't pick them up. Each one was about half full of change. I just had to laugh.

I wanted to do something meaningful with all the change he'd collected. Children's Healthcare of Atlanta (CHOA) had long been one of his favorite charities. He thought that since we didn't have children of our own we should do something to help other children. Also, he had owned Aflac stock for many years and liked the company. The Aflac Cancer Center at CHOA seemed like the perfect place to donate Phil's change.

Jamie, the Development Director of CHOA, joyfully received all the little containers of coins and found a business that would sort them at no charge for the center. The total came to $740. That's a lot of pennies, nickels, dimes and quarters.

I was happy to make this donation in memory of Phil. Another tribute that'll have a lasting impact. One little act that helps me feel I've honored his life in some way.

There are many ways to honor people who have passed. Some build monuments, some plant a tree, some start charities, some get fancy grave-stones, others finish a project the loved one had started. It's important to find a way of honoring or memorializing your spouse in a way that feels right to you.

Grief Does Not Equal Love

There's a quote being posted around social media that I just hate. It says, "Grief is the last act of love we have to give those we loved. Where there is deep grief there was great love."

The reason it upsets me so is that many people take this to heart and believe that the deeper they loved the longer and more deeply they have to grieve. Staying stuck in grief for years doesn't serve a loved one's memory and certainly doesn't serve you!

Grief is a natural reaction to loss. It isn't about the person or thing you lost. It's about you. Your sadness in having to live without him or her. The measure of your grief isn't a measure of your love. Keeping grief alive isn't honoring them. Being able to live well, laugh again, and enjoy your own life does not mean you didn't love the one you lost. It just means you are not letting the tragedy in your life claim you both.

As I've said earlier, just because you have tragedy in your life doesn't mean your life has to be a tragedy. I'd prefer mine be a romantic comedy. Like the heroine in any good movie I'll figure out a way to move forward despite devastating loss.

A Legacy of Influence

"You're not the placeholder for a dead man." I remember the day my wise therapist told me this. I was telling her I thought I needed to keep Phil's legacy alive and make sure people didn't forget him.

"He left his own legacy," she said. "I attended the funeral. I heard the things his friends said about him," she continued. "He left a legacy of influence. It's alive in every person he knew."

Yes, Phil did that! He probably never thought about a legacy or did anything for any reason other than it was what he wanted or what he believed was the right thing to do. After his funeral many people told me of ways he'd helped them when they needed it. Others told of how he inspired or encouraged them just by the way he lived his life. A few people told me that they'd left his funeral after hearing Phil's close friends speak about him and reevaluated how they were living their own lives and questioned whether they were the kind of people that others would regard as highly. Yes, he'd left his own legacy.

A few months later I was contacted by the Tennessee Telephone Association. Phil was in the telecommunications business and the association members were his clients. They give an annual college scholarship and they wanted to give one in his memory. So touching that his customers would honor him that way. Knowing that Phil grew up in Tennessee they sent word to the high schools in his hometown and the surrounding area. They selected a remarkable young woman who happens to live near Phil's mother. His family didn't know her but was delighted to meet her and learn that she was a leader in her school and had a 4.0 grade point average. The scholarship was awarded at the association's annual meeting and golf tournament. His family, a few close friends, and I were invited to attend. I was asked to speak. I talked about his Legacy of Influence. It was such an honor for the family to see him remembered that way.

If you're still looking for ways to memorialize or honor your spouse, look around at the legacy they've already left for themselves. They may not have achieved fame or recognition but their legacy lives in you and all the people whose lives they've touched.

Letting Go of the Marriage

After the words ". . . the marriage ended in death" marinated in my mind for a while, I decided that I had been living as if married to a dead man rather than as a single woman. Phil had traveled a lot with work while we were married so I was accustomed to him being away. But the forever-ness of him being gone was difficult to handle. Some days I couldn't face knowing that I'd never see him again so I'd just pretend he was out of town.

I realized that in order to really move forward I had to let go of the marriage. I had to stop acting like I was married to someone who just wasn't around anymore. But how would I do that?

I wrote Phil a letter. Being able to express my feelings and having some action to solidify my intention made sense to me.

In the letter I told him how much I loved him and thanked him for loving me and choosing me for his wife. I thanked him for all the years, adventures, and happiness we'd shared. I told him that when I married "until death do us part" I'd somehow taken that to mean until my death, but now I realized that I had to go on without him.

I shared that I knew he would expect me to date and remarry. I know that's what he would do. His mother, who was widowed very young, had lovingly told me that she'll always consider me family but she expects me to date and remarry. I stated that I was now giving myself permission and know in my heart I'd had his all along—to let go of being married to him. Yes, I still love him but the heart can hold love for more than one; just as a mother loves more than one child.

I thanked him for sharing his life with me, signed it "Love always," sealed it with a kiss and let my marriage go.

I know that I'm a better person from having been married to Phil for seventeen years. He was the perfect husband for me. Will I find another to be the perfect one for this time in my life? I don't know but now I'm open to the possibility.

Widow/Widower: Relationship Status or Identity?

After adjusting to the fact that the marriage had ended, I came to terms with being identified as a widow.

"I did not want to be called a widow," a friend shared with me as we discussed the word. She'd been widowed a long time ago, remarried, and raised a family with her second husband. She told me about sharing her aversion to the word with her minister soon after her first husband had died.

"Being widowed is something that happened to you. It's not who you are," he told her, encouraging her to use the term "single" if that was more comfortable for her.

Many widowed people have strong feelings about the word. I remember feeling like I'd been doused with cold water the first time I heard anyone use that word to describe me. Strangely, I had the same feeling the first time Phil introduced me as "my wife." I guess changing status and labels always gives us pause.

To me "widow" is the box I check for marital status. I'm not "divorced." "Single" doesn't feel right as I was happily married for a long time. I don't believe "widow" defines me either. Sure it's a part of who I am. I'm a widow. I'm a woman. I'm a daughter. I'm a sister. I'm an aunt. I'm a Southerner. I'm a writer. All those things are part of who I am. None of them tells the whole story.

I have found that in social situations when someone asks if I'm married and I reply that I'm widowed it usually redirects the conversation where I don't think saying divorced does.

As I mentioned earlier, they do the pause, nod and "I'm sorry," head shake. Then they seem tentative as if the poor widow might break into sobs any moment.

Even now it's been years since Phil died but when the occasion rises for me to state my marital status people always react the same way. Sometimes when I just go on with the conversation they'll touch my arm and repeat, "I'm so sorry." Sometimes they ask how or when. It would be easier to just say "single." Except it doesn't feel honest.

On anything other than legal forms you can say "single" or "widowed," whichever feels best to you. I use "widowed," but thanks to the conversation with Tricia I do it being fully aware that it's something that happened to me. It's not who I am.

Uncoupling

A few years back a Hollywood couple was going through a highly public divorce and said they were having a "conscious uncoupling." (The media had some fun with that.) I found that after Phil died I needed to consciously let go of the marriage and accept that I wasn't married to a dead person. I could memorialize him and honor him and at the same time figure out how to navigate having been widowed.

• • •

CHAPTER 10

Without This Ring

"Okay, Myra, I'm gonna tell you what no one else will. It's time to take off the ring." My Irish-Italian, Chicago-native friend Mike can be so blunt! "You're reminding me of those old Italian women who never remarry and keep wearing their wedding rings."

It had been almost a year since Phil died and I hadn't removed my rings. In fact, when the funeral director handed Phil's wedding band to me at the funeral home I'd slipped it over my rings and begun wearing it too. I knew that Mike was right. They needed to come off. But not yet.

Removing the rings is a big deal for most widows and widowers. It's a visible sign that you're no longer married. Some move them to the right hand. Others never remove their rings and never even consider dating or thinking of themselves as no longer married. (See Chapter 9: Married to a Dead Person.) Some take the rings off some days and put them back on other days. That wasn't an option for me.

Some of you may read the following and use the old line popularized by Southern humorist Lewis Grizzard, "I don't believe I'd a told that!" But one of my favorite writers and mentors once told me, "The more personal the more universal." We all know that if you're dealing with something embarrassing, someone else is too, and hearing your story may help. So I'm telling my secret.

I couldn't get my wedding rings off. When Phil asked me to marry him and gave me an engagement ring it was a little tight. He said we could have it sized but I was already thirty-four years old and had figured I'd never find love. Now that I'd fallen in love with this amazing man and he'd given me a beautiful ring I wasn't letting it out of my sight. And if I could only lose that last ten pounds (that I was going to lose every year) the ring wouldn't be tight.

I never had it sized.

After we married I gained some weight. Then gained some more. After years of strict dieting while single, my body just couldn't take the good food, entertaining, and traveling that we were doing as a couple. Plus, it wasn't long after we married that I hit the stage of life where women tend to gain weight. I gained and lost, gained and lost, repeatedly. I did a slow one step back, two steps forward climb up the scale. All the while not taking my wedding rings off. I literally grew into my rings just as I grew into the role of wife.

My ring finger is smaller at the back than at the knuckle so it wasn't painful and the rings would move around on my finger. They just wouldn't come off. Not even with soap and water. I wasn't worried. They weren't cutting off my circulation and I had no reason to remove them. I cleaned them with toothpaste and a toothbrush or with jewelry cleaner and little jewelry brush while wearing them. I just prayed that I was never robbed and held at gunpoint with demands that I give up the rings. That would've been an ugly scene.

As I contemplated taking my wedding rings off I knew it would be one time. Once and forever. I told Mike (who had no idea I couldn't get the rings off) that I'd do it but just wasn't ready. I set the anniversary of Phil's death as the date I'd remove my rings.

One Friday night my bro-friend Mark and I decided to meet a couple other friends at a singles event. He hadn't done that much since his divorce and I hadn't been to anything like that since being widowed. We were glad to be each other's wingman. I knew that wearing my wedding rings to a single's event wouldn't look right. Fortunately for me, elastic-band, costume rings were quite popular at the time. And cheap. I found a big one that didn't look anything like a wedding ring. It had a raised area in the middle so it fit nicely on top of my wedding ring, camouflaging it. Mark, who is one of the least judgmental people I know, just laughed when I told him. "We all have stuff," he said. He even said that when I was ready he'd help me cut the rings off. I couldn't believe I was confessing such an embarrassing thing. I also couldn't believe I absolutely could not remove my rings. I'd tried all the tricks I knew.

A few weeks later I was getting ready to go somewhere and just decided it was time. No need to wait for a special date. I was home alone and just got the wire cutters and snipped each band and removed my wedding rings. Not feeling the ring on my finger seemed strange. Symbolic that I was accepting no longer being married. My finger looked bizarre, indented where the rings had been for over seventeen years. I placed my rings in a safe place and put a fashion ring in their place. Then I called both Mike and Mark to let them know I'd removed the rings. Silly but I just needed someone to know.

I thought I'd feel sad or at least somber when I took off the rings. I didn't. It felt more like I'd made a big step forward. I felt strong and calm.

Several years later I had my rings and Phil's ring combined in a new design for a "right-hand ring." Many widowed and divorced women have their rings redesigned. It's hard to make one solitary diamond look like anything other than a wedding band but the right hand indicates that it isn't.

Passing It On

A few years later, after I'd sold our house and moved into a condo, a friend introduced me to a widower. Like me, he'd lost his spouse to cancer, sold his home in the suburbs, and moved to a high-rise condo. In fact, it was only about a block away from mine.

We met for coffee a few times, shared our stories, and became friends. As usually happens with widowers, he began dating pretty soon. We met for coffee when he was in his first relationship and I noticed he was still wearing his wedding band.

"It's time to take the ring off," I told him gently. He looked at me sort of sheepishly telling me that he'd asked a fellow widower about it but the guy didn't give any advice.

"You don't want to be in an intimate situation with your new girlfriend and have her look down and see your ring," I said. I suggested that he put it away and decide what to do with it later. He might even want to save it to pass down to one of his sons or grandson. "Take your late wife's photos out of the bedroom, too" I added.

Later that evening he texted a simple, "Thank you!"

If you're dating and ready for a new relationship it's time to remove outward signs that indicate you're married. We don't stop loving the person we lost because they're gone and we meet, or are trying to meet, someone new. Of course, you'll likely tell your potential new romantic partner about your late spouse. You may show pictures and bring your date to any memorial events or places you routinely visit. You may mention your spouse in conversation about things you did or places you visited. You just don't want to make your new love feel that your deceased husband or wife is always with the two of you. Two is a couple. Three's a crowd. Even if one is only there in spirit.

Taking off the rings sounds so simple but it's a big step in embracing life as a single person rather than part of a couple. It's emotional, and some-times you need a gentle nudge. Some men and women, especially older ones, never remove their rings. That's okay. It's a personal choice. Those folks usually have also chosen not to date.

Taking off the ring is a lot more than taking off a pair of earrings or a watch. It's removing an outward symbol of being married. It's emotional. I recently met a widow who told me about a 'ring removal ceremony' with candles, music and a prayer. However you decide to do it, it's a big step. Breathe.

CHAPTER 11

• • •

Roam for the Holidaze

"I've always dreamed of spending a Christmas in London . . ." Ronda Rich, a writer friend, stated in her weekly newsletter. Without much thought I sent a reply, "I'm not doing anything this Christmas. Want to go?" And that's how I happened to spend the first Christmas after Phil's death in London. "New traditions" had become my theme as I faced birthdays and holidays after his passing.

Christmas was only about six months after Phil died and this was my first trip out of the country without him. Phil and I had been to London before and had traveled abroad during the holidays but not London at Christmas. Ronda was a great travel companion. She loves planning trips. Phil did too. I don't. She's good at directions and navigating the train system. Phil was too. I'm not. I can do that if I have to but it takes longer for me to get oriented and figure it all out. Sometimes I can't find my way out of a parking deck. Trains? We could end up on the Orient Express.

London was both familiar and new. It was cold but still lovely with holiday decorations and a festive feeling in the air. We went to the Churchill Museum. Phil would have loved that. We had tea at the Ritz. Phil wouldn't have been so excited about that. I knew he would be happy that I was traveling over the holidays, and although I was seeing places he and I had been together and thinking of what he'd think or say about all we did, it wasn't as sad as I would have been at home trying to do the usual holiday stuff.

We ate at both nice restaurants and traditional pubs. We walked around the city a lot seeing sites including Buckingham Palace, Big Ben, the London Eye, London Bridge, Trafalgar Square, Tower Bridge, and Piccadilly Circus. Many of these places I remembered visiting with Phil. Ronda and I each shared stories from previous London visits. I hope I didn't bore her too much with tales of when I was there with Phil.

We saw a movie and attended a Christmas Eve caroling service at a historical church. We had a nice Christmas Dinner at the hotel restaurant and just as we were about ready for dessert the fire alarm went off. Everyone had to vacate the building. Apparently a small fire had started somewhere in an upper floor. Since we hadn't planned on going outside we'd worn only our dressy holiday dinner clothes. Ronda didn't have her passport but I always keep mine on my person when traveling. (I've seen too many movies of people losing their passport and not being able to leave the country. It pays to be a little paranoid.)

As we went out into the hallway and headed toward the front exit, hotel employees were handing blankets to guests as they left the building. Ronda and I took one to share. It was beginning to rain softly. Not enough to put out a hotel fire but enough to get our hair wet. We huddled together under the non-waterproof blanket. We, along with hundreds of other hotel guests, were herded around the block and into the lobby of another hotel to wait until the building had been cleared by the fire department.

I've been in several hotels over the years when fire alarms went off. I'm always amazed at how quietly and calmly people move in mass to evacuate and later return as though it's an everyday occurrence. After what seemed a long while but probably wasn't since we were chatting the entire time, we were allowed back into the hotel. Everyone in the restaurant picked right back up where they left off. We ordered dessert and coffee before going to our rooms. Neither fire nor rain nor wet hair would keep us from our dessert!

When there is someone or something you need to get away from you can go somewhere they aren't but you can never go away from the absence of someone. Anywhere you go they are still absent. But being in a completely different place with a completely different routine made getting through the first Christmas without Phil more bearable. His memory was always with me but there were many other things to focus on so that made it easier than if I'd been doing the old routines.

Christmas Tree-Dition

Phil and I had one holiday tradition that I've carried forward each year.

Our first Christmas as a married couple, we had a "tree trimming" party and friends brought ornaments. Over seventeen years of marriage we collected ornaments from our travels and special ones to signify something significant for each year. A "first Christmas together" ornament with a photo from our first year of marriage. A Harley-Davidson ornament for the year we bought a new motorcycle. A "new home" ornament when we moved into a new house. Several ornaments from ski trips and a Santa playing golf.

Each year, early in December, we'd decorate the tree while listening to Trans-Siberian Orchestra and drinking wine. Once the tree was done we would sit in front of the fire, finish off the wine, admire our tree, and reminisce with stories brought to mind by various ornaments.

The first year after Phil's death I wasn't sure whether to put up a tree. Especially since I was going away the week of Christmas. My sister Cynthia and nephew Christopher were staying with me so Christopher agreed to help with the tree. It turns out he loves Trans-Siberian Orchestra, too. He listened patiently as I told him the story of each ornament. Then he added a couple NASCAR ornaments of his own. Cynthia gave me some adorable ornaments of chubby mermaids drinking Margaritas to commemorate our almost-weekly Friday night Mexican dinners. Adding their personal touches to the tree warmed my heart.

When I returned from London I brought back a Big Ben ornament. My heart was broken but I was moving forward, starting new traditions, and making new memories. Adding new ornaments was a good idea.

The year that I sold "our" house and moved into a condo I gave away my big artificial tree and most of the decorations except for the commemorative ornaments. I didn't know what my new life would look like but I figured a big tree, all by myself, would be a big hassle.

Then I met Josh. He lived in my building and, although I'm about the age of his mother, we quickly became friends. Josh loves to decorate and helped me arrange my new home. "Right here is where your Christmas tree should go," he said one day while standing in front of my window. "A slim tree would be perfect here," he continued. I told him about the special ornaments and my memory tree. He agreed to help decorate.

Soon we were shopping for a new slim tree and a few new decorations. I found some burgundy ribbon with animal print swirls. It's so "me!" Guess what? Josh likes Trans-Siberian Orchestra. He decorated the tree with the flair of an artist while we drank wine and I told him the story of each ornament I unwrapped. Here I'd thought the tree-trimming would be lonely in my new home and now, with a new friend, it was fun again.

The following year Josh brought a friend to help decorate. A few neighbors came to watch. We all oohed and ahhed at how beautifully they adorned the tree. They made a huge bow for the top with my animal print ribbon. We even changed the music this year and switched to something more modern that the guys liked. It was joyous.

As I look at the tree my eyes wander from ornament to ornament remembering where and when I bought each one. The more recent ones also signify bringing "our" old tradition forward into "my" new life. Old traditions blending with the new. Remembering the past, savoring the present, and looking forward to the future.

Birthdays

Phil's birthday was the day after mine. Same year. We were born only one day apart. Yes, I married a younger man. I was a cougar before it was cool!

We always celebrated our birthdays together, usually with a trip. The first birthday after he passed I went out of town alone. He and I had visited Sedona, Arizona together the year before he died and I felt compelled to go back. It helped that I had a friend living in Phoenix at the time. I flew there, visited with her a couple days, then we drove to Sedona together. She left the next morning for an out of town trip and I was in Sedona a few days alone.

I hadn't traveled alone in a long time but it seemed safe there. I drove around the town, hiked up Bell Rock and visited the beautiful Chapel of the Holy Cross. Famed architect Frank Lloyd Wright helped design this striking little chapel that has long been an architectural landmark for Sedona. From a distance it looks like a large cross nestled in the red rocks.

The chapel is open daily for tourists to enjoy. I went in to sit, pray, light a candle, and just enjoy the beauty and the extraordinary view. The memory of having been there with Phil made it feel even more like a sacred place. My last night in Sedona I drove to the small airport which boasts the city's best views of the sunset.

The time alone in such a transcendent setting was very healing. I rested, relaxed, treated myself to a massage, and spent some time journaling about my sadness, about missing Phil, about the peace and serenity I felt there and about what I was doing each day.

Since that first birthday after Phil's death I usually plan something special for myself on those days. It seemed strange celebrating my birthday alone since it was so connected to Phil's. It's difficult to explain but since Phil and I always celebrated together it seems personal and private.

Many of my single friends celebrate their birthdays with parties or special lunches or dinner with friends. Some celebrate "birthday week" with a variety of events with different friends. They seem to expect me to do the same. I've discouraged them from calling any attention to my birthday. I don't put it on Facebook. Birthday cards are nice— Hallmark "for those who care enough to send the best"— and birthday texts for those who care only enough to do the very least.

Some haven't understood that I don't want to get together to celebrate. Some have pressured me to get together for a birthday lunch or dinner. Even if I go out of town they want to celebrate before I leave or after I return. One year when I was feeling particularly pressured to celebrate I said to a friend, "What I'd really like is for my friends to support me in celebrating my birthday in my own private way." That seemed to take care of it.

Usually I spend the two days writing, seeing movies, getting a massage, or taking a drive. Just time alone pampering myself and contemplating my life. Last year I did go to a play with a close friend. Maybe someday I'll want to celebrate my birthday partying with others. Until then it's a good time for remembering, reflecting, and planning the next year.

I recommend that you decide how you want to celebrate your birthday and that of your late spouse. Just plan it. Even if what you want is to be alone. Deciding and planning how you'll spend the day helps you to feel more in control than planning nothing, dreading it, and then feeling sorry for yourself because he or she isn't there to be with you. Yes, it seems strange and sad to have to plan your own birthday celebration if you're used to having someone to celebrate with but lots of single, divorced, and widowed people do it.

If you prefer to be with friends and no one reaches out, then reach out to someone. Tell your friends what you'd like to do or where you'd like to go. Invite someone over for dinner. Go to a movie. Go to a museum or botanical garden. Get a massage. Throw yourself a party. If you have children, the little ones can help you blow up the balloons or the older ones can take you out to dinner. If they don't offer, then ask. Many single, divorced, or widowed people I know let their friends know weeks in advance, "My birthday is coming up and here's what I want to do . . ." Friends are always glad to celebrate. If yours aren't, as one of my friends says, "It's time to thin the herd." Get out your list and get some fun new friends.

If money is an obstacle, check the website for the local universities. They often have free or low cost movie screenings and concerts. Go for a walk or to a church service. If you're staying home then plan a nice dinner and bubble bath. You can even buy individual cupcakes with one candle. I can't say I recommend making or buying yourself a whole cake unless you have children or live with family. A whole cake at my house would be, well, five more pounds to lose.

The key is planning something that makes you feel good and brings you joy. If you can't bear the thought of getting out of the house then I recommend a movie marathon. If you don't have Netflix or On Demand, see if your local library has movies you can check out. A good book is another way to spend a day of solitude and a novel can be a great escape.

Anniversaries

The anniversary of Phil's death is two days before our wedding anniversary. The first few years after he passed I blocked those days off on my calendar and spent them alone. Several times I watched the video from his funeral and listened to the recording of the speakers, spending time with his memory since I couldn't be with him.

Seeing the video, which is a collection of photos of his life, and hearing the stories people told about him reminds me of what an amazing person he was and the life we had together. It made me happy I'd had a life with him. Being sad because I missed him was always there too.

The anniversary dates aren't times when others expect me to be out celebrating so isolating myself is pretty easy. Now that several years have passed I usually just say a prayer of thanksgiving for having shared many years with him and then go on as if it's an average day. That wasn't easy to do in the beginning and taking the time to grieve privately suited me well. Although I did sometimes invite Ben & Jerry. Or Jose.

On Facebook I often see where a widow or widower posts a wedding photo or photo of their spouse and notes the anniversary. This is a simple way to acknowledge it and share the memory if that's what feels good to you. Friends won't likely mention it if you don't as they don't know what to say and whether you want anyone mentioning it. If you prefer not to mention it and just get through the day without anyone else bringing it up, that's your choice.

Valentine's Day

Phil always brought me a dozen roses on Valentine's Day. Brought. They weren't delivered. He thought that was too extravagant. Every Valentine's Day he would stop by the grocery store on his way home and pick up a dozen roses. I'd make dinner. We'd exchange cards and have a romantic evening at home.

The first Valentine's Day after he passed I still felt surrounded with love. I missed him but chose to focus on the love of my friends and family and the happy memories of Valentine's Days past. (Note: I'm not saying it was easy!)

My sister gave me a single rose and a card. My nephew brought a sweet card and box of candy. What surprised me most was that three of Phil's buddies called me. Two gave lame excuses for calling but I knew they just wanted to know that I was okay. The other was upfront. "It's Valentine's Day and I wanted to check on you," Mike called before taking his wife to dinner. "Do something fun and don't be sad," he said.

Of course I missed my husband and grieved that he was no longer with me. Valentine's Day is for couples and I was no longer part of a couple. Still, I was surrounded by love. Not romance. Love. Caring. Friendship. I gave thanks for those types of love that are especially important in the absence of romantic love!

That day I decided to always celebrate Valentine's Day with flowers. I could choose to be sad because I was alone or I could choose to celebrate the happy marriage I'd had and the love of family and friends that is still in my life.

I've found that buying myself flowers spreads joy to others too. The first Valentine's Day that I put a dozen roses on the grocery checkout counter, the cashier said cheerfully, "You're about to make someone happy!"

"They're for me," I laughed.

"Good for you!" she said enthusiastically. The lady in line behind me agreed. They shared a smile and loved my story about buying flowers for myself now that my husband is gone. I posted a photo of the flowers on Facebook and friends made happy comments. Maybe it gives others permission to give themselves flowers too.

Many single, divorced, and widowed friends confess that Valentine's Day is difficult for them. Some openly hate it. Sometimes they stress over it and refuse to go out and face restaurants filled with couples. Would I like to have romance? Sure. But I do have love. Why not celebrate that on Valentine's Day? It sure beats sitting home feeling blue.

In the years that I've been widowed I've celebrated at home with my flowers, a movie, and chocolates. I've gone with a friend to a casual restaurant for early dinner around 5:30 and sat at the bar. (By the way, that's where you find single guys on February 14th.) One year I went to a play with a girlfriend. Another year I went with a group of gals to see a movie that released on Valentine's Day.

Valentine's Day doesn't have to be sad. Find someone else who may be feeling unloved and do something fun with them. Look around and see all the love in your life and celebrate that. Love of your children and family. Love of friends. Love of your pets. Love of Chunky Monkey. (Hey, it's a one-time splurge, OK?) Love of what brings you joy.

Firsts Are the Worst

The first year of anything without your love will most likely be challenging. First birthday, first Christmas or Hanukkah, first anniversary of his or her death, first Father's or Mother's day, birthdays of your children, first Valentine's Day, first New Year. These are things you can plan for or at least brace yourself for because you know they're coming up.

The unexpected or unplanned things were worse for me. My knees almost buckled the first time I went to the drug store where I always bought his medications. The grocery store was the same way. I would see all the things that could help or comfort him before and now he wasn't around.

About six months after he passed I went to the dry cleaners to drop off some clothes. They handed me some of Phil's shirts that had been there so long I'd forgotten about them. I cried all the way home.

Someone once told me that it takes a full year to see all the holes the death of a loved one has left in your life. Sometimes holes show up even later than that.

A year or so ago I was encouraging my mama to buy a new car. Although hers was old, had a lot of miles, and was beginning to need repairs, she was reluctant to get rid of it. One day I took her out to some dealerships to look around and as we were driving she said, "Buster always bought the cars."

Then I realized that although Daddy had been gone for about six years it was another "first" for her. We talked about how Daddy loved to trade cars. He enjoyed looking and the negotiation process. Mama is emotionally strong and has always been independent. She didn't show much emotion or cry in front of anyone when Daddy passed. She just got on with life. This was one of the few times I'd ever heard her sound sad about him being gone. Phil was diagnosed with a brain tumor only six months after Daddy died so the first birthday, Christmas, and Father's Day after Daddy passed was overshadowed by Phil's illness and later by his death.

I assured Mama that Cynthia and I had done lots of online research and I'd test drive with her and handle the negotiation. She was okay with that but I know it didn't take away the sadness that Daddy wasn't there for it. Giving up the last car he bought was losing another piece of him and their life together. Once she found a vehicle she liked and we made the trade I told her that I thought Daddy would be proud of us and would like the new car. After all, it was a Cadillac. Daddy always thought it wasn't really a car if it wasn't a Cadillac!

New Traditions

New things, new people, new places, new routines—all are part of moving forward. So is letting go of the old. Or altering them in some way. If you know something is coming up that'll be difficult, make a plan. Invite someone to join you or help you. Plan something special for yourself on the date or after the occasion. It does get easier with time.

They say, "Time heals all wounds."

"Time heals nothing," says psychologist Phil McGraw, PhD. "It's what you do with that time that makes things change." I think he's right. It helped me to consciously choose to work toward happiness and to plan around upcoming things I knew would bring pain.

Holidays, birthdays, anniversaries, Valentine's Day—they'll never be the same. They can still be good.

• • •

CHAPTER 12

What's the Speed Limit for Moving On?

"I'm just worried that you are not moving on quickly enough," a friend said after a little too much wine. She was one of my dearest friends and had come to visit and spend the night. "My other friend who lost her husband is married already," she continued.

The anger boiled inside me as the words scorched my mind. We'd known each other for so many years, she seems like family, and I knew she had my best interest at heart. That's the only reason we're still friends today.

I'd had enough wine that my inhibitions were low and what she said hurt so much. I lashed out, "Yes, she put another man into the missing husband's slot. She's still in the same job, same house, and has the same friends," I blustered. "When you've lost your husband, given up your job, learned to handle another business, sold a house, and purchased another then you can tell me how to move on. Until then I'd appreciate it if you didn't!"

"Oh, Myra! I'm so sorry!" She hugged me. "I just worry about you and want you to be happy again." She went on to tell me that a mutual friend who sees me more often had told her I talk about Phil too much.

That was like another slap in the face. It had only been a couple years at this point. Was I not supposed to mention him? He was part of almost every memory I had from the last seventeen years. Places "we'd" visited, things "we'd" done, and people "we" know. It would be awhile before I could make enough 'me' memories to replace those. How did she not get that?

I knew that she did care and was hurting for me. I just told her I thought it was time we went to bed. The next morning we had a pleasant visit before she left. We never mentioned moving forward again.

After she left I called my widow-sister Cynthia. (Not to be confused with birth-sister Cynthia.) She soothed the pain and told me that I was doing fine and no one has the right to tell anyone how or how fast to move on. There are just some things only someone who's walked the same road understands.

Your Grief Is Unique to You

Most widows and widowers have a story about someone who has told them they are moving on too fast or too slowly. Here are some examples:

- The clueless co-worker who notices you're having a bad day and says, "That was months ago. I thought you'd be over it by now."

- The caring longtime friend who chides you for dating "too soon," not understanding that you crave companionship and that doesn't mean you didn't love your wife.

- The always-partnered friend who thinks "moving forward" means getting into a new relationship, therefore, if you aren't dating you're stuck in grief.

- The new friend who notices that you still display photos of your late spouse and asks when you're going to take them down.

- The one who thinks not displaying photos means you no longer think of your spouse.

Most of the comments about moving on too quickly or too slowly come while you're still emotionally fragile. Most recent widows/widowers are too wounded to stand up for themselves and assertively put the offender in his or her place. That doesn't mean I recommend the harsh, aggressive way I handled it. Just don't take it too personally. How can they get it when they haven't experienced such a loss?

There's no timeline for moving on. The first day that you are bathed, dressed, and walk outside your door you are moving forward. Don't let anyone tell you that you are not. If you show up at work unbathed, with dirty hair, and wearing your bunny slippers and bathrobe you may need a little help.

As with any emotional problem the signs to look for are time and intensity. Sobbing every day the first month seems reasonable to me. If you're still sobbing every day the seventh month you may want to see your doctor or go to a grief group or therapist. If your eyes moisten a bit when you hear your favorite song two years later that's okay. Time may have passed but the intensity isn't out of line.

As long as you are able to function, anyone other than your closest friends and family should mind their own business. Even close friends and family should tread lightly.

If you lost your leg no one would expect you to "get over it." Yes, they'd expect you to move forward. They'd give you some time to heal and to learn to function with only one leg. They'd expect you to eventually get over the grief, anger, self-pity, or whatever you're feeling. They would expect that eventually how you're managing would not be the topic of every conversation. They wouldn't expect you to never mention it again.

Recently there have been a couple contestants on *Dancing with the Stars* that are amputees. No one would say these inspirational and accomplished people haven't moved forward with their lives. At the same time, no one would expect them to pretend they hadn't lost a leg or arm. They discuss the challenges of adapting dance steps to their personal situations. They aren't there to pretend it never happened. Their presence and showing what they can do despite the loss inspires others.

When I first lost Phil I tried to find a little sliver of joy and something to be grateful for in each day. Some days the grief won. Soon there were more than just moments of joy; there could be whole hours! Eventually there were days and then weeks. Now I feel good most of the time. Occasionally a memory or event will still make me sad but it doesn't take me to my knees.

There's a lovely quote by Henry James that says, "Sorrow comes in great waves . . . but it rolls over us, and though it may almost smother us it leaves on the spot and we know that if it is strong we are stronger inasmuch as it passes and we remain."

As long as you're still standing and functioning in your life, don't listen to anyone who tells you that you are moving too slowly or too quickly. If they don't like your pace they can walk with someone else!

• • •

CHAPTER 13

Sifting through Memories and Discarding Dreams

"So why did these people put so much money in the basement and not remodel the kitchen?" My real estate agent relayed this question from a potential buyer for our house. Yes, modernizing the kitchen was the next project on our list. Sadly, the brain tumor diagnosis came just as we finished putting an Irish pub in our basement. We never got to the kitchen update. Creating a big kitchen designed for entertaining was just one dream I had to discard.

I put "our" house on the market a couple years after Phil died. We'd moved in only two-and-a-half years before he was diagnosed. Moving into the house was so much fun. Well, moving wasn't actually fun but getting into a new house, decorating it, and making it our own was. Sifting through all the stuff we bought for the new house as well as all the stuff we'd collected over the years brought up lots of memories. I sifted through the memories, too.

"How important is it to you that we get a new house?" Phil asked when we were engaged. I told him it wasn't. He had a nice house. We were both traveling for work and house hunting was a big job. Plus, we could live in his bachelor house for a while and then figure out where we wanted to move. I had no idea we'd stay there thirteen years. When we decided to move we looked at houses for about six months before finding the right one. We planned to live there at least until we retired. He planned to retire early so we estimated we'd live there about 10 years. Four years later he was dead.

The new house was only a few miles from our old one but it was newer, bigger, and on an acre of land in a nice neighborhood. It was a great house for entertaining. We immediately started projects. Phil loved projects.

He worked with the builder to design it all just as he wanted. He added a roof to the existing porch and screened it in. He picked out all the paint, stain, planks, tiles, and ceiling fan. He added a new deck, moving the existing outside staircase to free up the view from the unfinished basement. He worked with an ironsmith to design a black wrought iron railing to surround it all and bought nice patio furniture and a big gas grill. The space was lovely and the porch became our favorite room in the house.

Next we discussed redoing the outdated kitchen and finishing the basement. He decided to do the basement first. A bathroom was already finished there. He wanted an Irish pub, a TV room, and an additional bedroom. That would still leave an unfinished area as storage since the basement was the full footprint of the house.

Again he worked with the builder to design what looked like an authentic Irish Pub. A brick fireplace was already there. He added a bar, complete with brass farmhouse style sink, refrigerator, dishwasher and a kegerator. There were two corner sitting areas, a built-in wine rack, and, of course, a big screen TV. The space had dark wood on the floor, halfway up the walls, and on the coffered ceiling. The builder found four small lion heads made of some sort of plaster. He stained them to match the wood and mounted them on columns so they looked like they were carved from the wood. Glass shelves on the mirrored wall behind the bar were lined with glasses, liquor, and assorted other libations. The finishing touch was a neon light saying, "McElhaney's Irish Pub." It was a sight to behold.

The adjoining room had a brick floor in a hounds tooth pattern and brick walls halfway up. The walls above were dark green. The large brown corduroy sectional sofa from Phil's bachelor days was situated in front of another big screen TV.

The extra bedroom? Well, it just had a bed and curtains. Phil's buddies loved the idea of sleeping just steps away from the pub!

Phil thoroughly enjoyed every step of designing and creating the pub. He worked closely with the builder and after every business trip he was eager to get to the basement to see what had been done in his absence. The finishing touches were just being done when he received the devastating diagnosis. He went ahead and had a stone patio put in under the porch and just outside the pub.

So, we didn't get around to updating the kitchen. It was a dream I'd just have to discard. The possible options we had discussed would be something we'd never act on. Creating the pub and the parties we had in it during the eighteen months between diagnosis and death were precious memories I'll always share with friends and family.

Phil's touch and presence was all over our house so it's easy to see why selling it and moving was the most difficult thing I faced after he died.

What About All the Stuff?

Anyone who has ever moved knows what it's like to go through every piece of your stuff, deciding where it should go. Downsizing is more difficult because not as much of your stuff, lovingly collected (or unwittingly accumulated) over the years, will fit into the new place. Having to downsize so soon after we'd upsized reminded me of an old George Carlin routine.

"That's all your house is, a place to keep your stuff," Carlin says. "While you go out and get more stuff." He continues on a hilarious rant about getting, storing, and moving stuff. "Sometimes you gotta move. Why? Too much stuff!" And then when you move into a bigger house you buy more stuff to fill the space. Crazy!

We had stuff! Dealing with all the stuff was a big headache when I was preparing to sell the house. My sister and nephew had lived with me temporarily but they'd already moved out and taken their stuff. I staged the house to sell and stored a lot of stuff. I cleaned and threw away a lot of stuff. But there was so much more stuff. Sometimes I wondered if our stuff was getting frisky and giving birth to more stuff.

Phil and I had kept the house relatively neat and clean. I would have sworn that we were not hoarders but I was amazed at what I found while cleaning out the house. When you have room for storage—several closets and an unfinished part of a basement—it's so easy to just take a box and put it out of sight to deal with later.

I found boxes of stuff Phil had long before we met, including photos, letters, concert tickets, ski lift tickets, and pay stubs from the late 1970's when he was working his way through college. Yep! Had to keep those. Never knew when I might need to prove my income and deductions from thirty years ago. Looking through stuff he had before we married reminded me of many stories he told about his childhood growing up with four brothers, college years partying with friends and when he was a young man starting his career.

I wasn't too bad about keeping stuff I didn't need. Except for one room. I work from home and my office was upstairs. There was an unfinished area off my office. The roof sloped so it couldn't be used for anything but storage. My office was always cluttered since I tend to keep stuff in piles rather than organized files. Oh, I have the files, and they're labeled. I just keep stuff out where I can see it.

It's embarrassing to admit but I discovered that I was hoarding office supplies. File folders, labels, envelopes, sticky notes, markers, paper clips. All the stuff that can keep you organized. I keep buying them thinking if I had enough I'd somehow magically become organized. There was an old computer that no longer worked. One of the big ones no one uses anymore. Cords that went to nothing. Cords intertwined with other cords. Gadgets with no cords. Bundles of workbooks and program handouts for programs I hadn't taught in years. Oh, and let's not forget the VHS tapes. Wouldn't want to lose those.

These things brought back memories of all the years I'd spent building my speaking and training business. The business I'd put on hold when Phil was diagnosed. Would I go back to my business or was it just a memory, too? As I chose what to keep and what to discard I wasn't sure. I held on to some stuff just in case

I cleared out a lot of junk. Trashed a lot and donated a lot. Packed up a lot to move with me. Going through boxes of old stuff I cried regularly. There were projects started that now would never be finished. Books about places we planned to visit. Trips that we'd never take together. Things we'd planned to do together. Someday. Dreams that now had to be discarded.

We'd never build that fire pit in the back yard. The travel guides Phil had been reading about Croatia wouldn't be used on our next trip. We'd never replace that old carpet. He'd never enjoy the retirement he'd planned so carefully for. We'd never spend that month in Ireland he'd dreamed of. There were boxes and albums of photos of Phil's lifetime, from his college years and throughout our marriage. Souvenirs of places we'd been and things we'd done.

His racquetball trophies reminded me of our early years together when he played competitively. The top salesman awards reminded me of the sales incentive trips that took us to Switzerland, Australia, and Hawaii. I boxed up the scrapbooks I'd made of annual ski vacations and trips to Europe. The New Year's Eve decorations could be tossed as we'd no longer host those parties. I could take the crystal and the china cabinet but the dining room would never again be filled with extended family for a holiday dinner. I kept the Harley boots but would never be on the back of his motorcycle again. So many memories to sift through as I decided what I could take to my new home.

One thing I stressed over was Phil's trophies. He had numerous awards for sales achievements, a few plaques for serving as an officer in Toastmasters, and several trophies for racquetball competitions. What would I do with things like that? I wouldn't have room for all of them in my new place, wherever that was. We didn't have children to pass them down to. I doubted any of his brothers would want them sitting around. I didn't want to donate plaques and trophies with his name on them. Thrift stores couldn't sell those, could they?

About this time Oprah Winfrey's *O Magazine* event was coming to the World Congress Center in Atlanta. I invited sister-Cynthia to go with me. It was a huge convention-type event where we saw Gayle King, Suzie Orman, Dr. Oz, Nate Berkus, and Peter Walsh. This was the last year of her TV talk show so she didn't always attend the magazine event. We got a great surprise. Oprah was the closing speaker! It was a fun day for Cynthia and me to hear all the speakers, seeing them in person after years of seeing them on TV. Plus, we got to be in the room with Oprah. Of course, there were a few thousand others there too and hundreds between us and the stage. Still, we were in the room with Oprah Winfrey! We heard her speak and there were swag bags filled to the brim with all sorts of stuff. Those bags alone were worth the price of the tickets.

At the end of the day we saw author Peter Walsh heading out the door. He's known for helping people organize and reduce clutter. People were stopping him to take photos. I walked up to him saying I had one question. I told him that I'd lost my husband and was cleaning out stuff in our house but didn't know what to do with his trophies. Saying it, tears filled my eyes. He hugged me, took my hands, and looked into my eyes.

"I know one thing," Mr. Walsh said. "Your husband would not want this. He would not want you to be standing here crying over stupid trophies."

He told me to keep three, take the rest somewhere with friends and a bottle of wine and bury them. I waved Cynthia up and introduced her to him. Mr. Walsh was so kind and caring in those few short moments. What he said seemed to free me. And he was right. Phil wouldn't want me to be crying and stressing our over stupid stuff.

I decided to keep only one. A crystal replica of the Sydney Opera House that Phil received as a President's Club sales award, along with a trip to Australia where we toured the opera house and learned of its history. I talked with one of his brothers soon afterward and it turned out that he wanted the trophies to keep in memory of Phil. I gave all the rest to him.

Gotta Get Outta This House

There was a slump in home sales and the house was on the market for a total of seven months. "Our" beautiful, happy house and no one wanted it. I was worrying about everything. The timing if someone made an offer and I hadn't yet found a new home; how to know what to keep if I didn't yet know where I was moving and what would fit into the new place; how long I could keep making house payments on that big house if it didn't sell soon. Plus, how much time would I have between the offer and closing to figure out what to do with all the furniture I wasn't taking but needed to keep in the house for staging?

Our happy house had begun to feel like a big burden. During the two years between Phil's death and the sale of the house I had to replace one of the hot water heaters. A pipe burst in the yard and had to be dug up and replaced. A tree fell on the neighbor's fence during a storm and damaged it so I had to repair the fence and have the tree removed. The roof had to be replaced. The heating system went out and had to be replaced.

While the house was on the market the power shut down and a repair had to be made in the power box on the outside of the house. Somehow this required involving an electrician and the city officials issuing some sort of permit. I'm still shaking my head over that one. I was having nightmares of Tom Hanks 1980's comedy, *The Money Pit*.

An animal of some sort, probably a squirrel, died in the attic. The handyman I called went into the attic but couldn't find a critter body to remove. Despite all my cleaning and investments in sprays, smell removal products, candles, and room fresheners, plus opening windows and using fans in the summer heat; prospective home buyers were greeted with the fragrance of dead rodent. Plus an outdated kitchen. I dropped the price.

After looking at a few condos I found one I liked but couldn't make an offer because the house hadn't sold. I decided to hold off on looking because I didn't want to fall in love with another one and not be able to get it. I kept looking online and drove around various areas of town, narrowing down where I wanted to live. Months later I still wasn't getting offers on the house. I walked around it and prayed. I thanked the house for providing a beautiful, happy place for us to live and entertain friends and family. I told it I needed to let it go and maybe a wonderful young family would move in and fill its rooms with laughter. I wrote a letter to place on the kitchen counter with the Realtor's brochure. It was cheerful and upbeat. I thanked potential buyers for looking at the house and told them it was a happy house that had been filled with family, friends, love, and laughter and that, although it was time for me to move on, it would be a good home for them.

My Realtor suggested that I start looking at condos because knowing what was out there would make it easier to let go of the house. He told me which neighborhood in our school district and price range was our biggest competition in attracting buyers. I drove through it and realized the houses and lawns looked nicer and the neighborhood was larger for the same money. I called Ted, the friend I go to with financial questions, to discuss it. He talked to me about what I was spending on the mortgage and upkeep of the house. With his input I decided that even lowering the price again and losing money on the house was the best decision. I could cut my expenses and move on to my new place. It was time.

I called the Realtor and told him to drop it like it's hot. He didn't seem to think that was funny. I thought it meant to drop something quickly, like the phrase "drop it like a hot potato." Later I learned it was a hip-hop dance phrase that means something totally different and a little nasty. Oops! We dropped the price again. Like a hot potato. I began an earnest search for my new home.

By this time I'd narrowed my search down to an in-town area. The real estate broker I'd been working with had one of his young agents look at condos with me. She and I had fun seeing the different buildings and units in the area I'd selected. We swapped links to places that were available, discussed them, and went out several days to see some in person. We probably looked at eight or nine condos.

Finally I got an offer on my house! It was a young couple with a little girl. They asked if it would be possible to push the closing back a couple months. Great! This would give me more time to get rid of furniture and find a place to live.

A few weeks later Cynthia sent an email with a link announcing an open house in three buildings in the area where I'd been looking. I didn't know she'd been doing some research to help me find a home. I told her I'd already looked at the ones that were in my price range but I'd go to the open house anyway.

One was in the building where my agent and I had looked at several condos. One of them was currently at the top of my list. I liked the building, the location, and the price was right, but the unit needed updating so I didn't love it. I didn't need a zillion more decisions to make like picking counter tops, carpets and commodes. Nope! Deciding where to put my leopard print chairs would be stressful enough.

The open house in that building had three condos to view. One was small and dreary. Another was a penthouse that was way out of my price range. The other was the right size but still over my price range. As we went up the elevator the agent said it had been on the market almost two years with no offer so if I was interested not to let the price hold me back from making an offer. As the Realtor said, the housing slump works both ways. I'd lose money on my house and get a good deal on a condo.

I couldn't believe the view! It was amazing and had floor-to-ceiling windows. I loved it! We hadn't found it before because it was above the price range we were searching for. If not for Cynthia sending the link about the open house I would have missed this fabulous condo.

I called my agent and told her about it, saying I wanted her to see it. I was afraid that maybe I'd been blinded by the view and didn't get a realistic assessment of the condo. On second look I liked it even better. The kitchen and bathrooms were fully upgraded with cabinets and countertops. Nice crown molding and good layout. And, of course, the floor-to-ceiling windows and great view.

I made an offer. It was accepted with little negotiation. The owners wanted a few months to close so the timing worked out well. I had one week between the closing on our house and the closing on my condo. A week that I easily arranged to spend with friends.

The story gets better. Not only did the condo have everything I wanted (other than carpet when I prefer hardwoods) but the timing was perfect. The selling real estate agent told me that she'd scheduled to have a professional photographer come the week after the open house to take better photos. If the photos on the listing had truly shown the beauty of the upgrades and view it would have been snapped up before I saw it.

The building has a parking deck. I have an aversion to parking decks and have been known to leave them without parking if I can't get a space where I can see my car from the elevator. I guess I've watched too many movies and nothing good ever happens in parking decks. My friend Gayle used to tease me about it. She said, "Nothing's going to happen to you. Unless you hear that scary music!" I figured that if I was going to live in a high rise I'd just have to get over my fear and trust that it was safe. Once I made an offer and got all the information on the condo, I found that my deeded parking space was the second one from the door to the elevator. How cool is that? I like to think Phil had a little something to do with me finding the perfect place with the close parking space. Phil and Cynthia working together to take care of me.

Making the Move

Having a month before the couple wanted to close on our house and a little longer before the closing for my new condo gave me time to move. The timing of that was one of my biggest worries and it seemed to fall into place.

Now that I knew the dimensions of my new place I could make final decisions on what furniture I'd take with me. A few family members and friends were taking some furniture and a friend of a friend who was recently divorced was buying the rest. One friend said I could store the things I was taking in his basement until I took possession of my condo. That took care of paying storage fees. Another couple invited me to stay at their home during the week between closing on our house and taking possession of my new condo. That took care of another worry.

I'd cleared out a lot of stuff during the time the house was on the market and I thought I'd done a good job of getting things packed and ready to go. Until I really got into it. Then it seemed like everything multiplied. My stuff had begat more stuff again. Every time I thought I was finished with a room there would be another closet or drawer that I'd find hadn't been touched. Even with all I'd given away or sold there was still too much, plus all the little stuff I hadn't paid much attention to. Way too many dishes, utensils, pots, and pans for my smaller condo that had to be sorted through. I no longer needed all the bed linens I'd used in a big house with lots of guest rooms or the tools Phil had collected over the years. The more stuff I cleared out the more stuff appeared. I was physically and emotionally exhausted when I got a call from my sister asking if I needed her to come and help. Hallelujah! She was in the midst of changing jobs and had a week off between them just when I needed her. Had Cynthia not come and helped me finish with all the packing and clearing out I'd probably still be sitting there between boxes crying.

The day the movers came we worked late into the evening. I spent the night with a friend and sobbed myself to sleep. I was emotionally and physically depleted. I was saying "goodbye" to the life Phil and I had known and moving on into the unknown. I knew where I'd be living but not much of anything else.

The next morning I awoke early and went back to the house. Cynthia met me there. We did the final walk-through and hauled out trash and cleaned out the refrigerator. The cleaning crew came and was still there when the couple buying the house did their final walk-through.

At the closing I was barely holding myself together. Then the lawyer handed me a paper to sign saying that my husband was deceased, leaving me as sole owner. I signed it, excused myself, and went into the bathroom so they wouldn't see me cry.

Looking back I wish I'd had an estate sale company come and handle the disposal of all our stuff. Even with their commission I'm sure I'd have made more money on what I sold and had so much less stress in clearing out everything.

A week with friends, Larry and Susan, was a great respite from leaving the house. They're retired and she's calm and thoughtful with caring energy. They have a beautiful home on the river with a sunroom that's the perfect place to curl up with a book. I rested a lot. She made dinner some nights and others we went out. It was very peaceful and a great haven for me to retreat from the outside world for a while.

The day before the movers were scheduled to deliver my furniture to the new condo I got a call from the real estate agent saying the previous owners had finished moving out and I could take possession of my condo at 5 p.m. that day. I was eager to get into it and decided to go down and spend the night in my new home, even without furniture.

As I drove down to the condo I thought, "If I were writing a movie, this is where it would end." My old life in the rear-view mirror and the unknown up ahead.

But I wasn't writing a movie. It was my life and I was leaving behind a life I loved. Would I be able to build a new life I could love? I didn't know. I felt more trepidation than excitement.

I stopped by the Target a block from the condo and bought an inflatable air mattress to use as a bed. I needed one for future guests anyway. At the grocery store next door I picked up a small bottle of champagne. Might as well toast the beginning of my new life alone.

I carried the mattress, champagne and my suitcase into my new, empty condo. That's when I realized I didn't have linens for the mattress. Or towels, soap, and shampoo to bathe. Or a champagne glass. I sat on the floor with my champagne looking out the floor-to-ceiling windows at the beautiful nighttime view of the city. I'd sifted through all the reminders of the wonderful memories of my life with Phil. I'd discarded the dreams of all the things we'd planned. Now I was here alone to build a new life.

What did the future hold for me? I had no clue. When it was time for bed, I pulled clothes out of my suitcase to use as a cover on the bare inflatable mattress. I was overwhelmed with loneliness.

The next day the movers brought my furniture to my new home. Having my own furniture in the new condo felt like old friends coming into the unfamiliar place with me. My bedroom now held my bed so I had a good place to sleep. It was the only thing in the room . . . the dining room was too full with the table and china cabinet I'd brought from the old house. The living room had only the basics. I'd gotten rid of a house full of furniture and now needed to buy new things for my new place. That seemed such a waste but the big stuff wouldn't work in my little condo. The extra bedroom that would eventually become my office was just the transitory spot for boxes and anything I wasn't sure where to put. It felt like another big job to tackle but at the same time it was like turning the page to a new chapter. Would it be a good chapter? Only time would tell. I was relieved not to have the responsibility of the big house with the big yard. I didn't know what my new life held. I felt a mix of excitement and uncertainty. Mostly uncertainty. And dread at having to unpack all those boxes.

Old Memories and New Dreams

Joseph Campbell says, "We must be willing to let go of the life we planned so as to have the life that's waiting for us." He didn't say it'd be easy.

As I sifted through my stuff and the memories they held, I had to let go of a lot of the objects but I'll always have the memories. While letting go of things, I mourned for "our" dreams that we'd never see fulfilled. It was sad. I grieved for the life I'd planned. It took a while but now I'm making new dreams and memories and looking forward to the life that's waiting for me.

• • •

CHAPTER 14

Feeling Frisky

"Actually that's natural. Your body is reawakening," my therapist explained. I confessed to her that soon after my husband died, all I could think about was sex. That just seemed wrong. "For over eighteen months now you've been so focused on taking care of Phil and then dealing with his death that you stopped thinking about your own needs." She was right. Although Phil and I had a good sex life for our seventeen years of marriage I'd hardly thought about it for the last few months of his life. As the treatments took their toll he was increasingly tired. Eventually he needed full-time care and although we were always loving and affectionate, sex wasn't in the picture near the end. I was hyper-focused on caring for him and sort of numb to what my body needed anyway. Sex, rest, exercise, nutrition, recreation—none of that was urgent. Caring for Phil was my top priority.

After he was gone I still loved him and the thought of sex with another man made me shudder. Still, I longed to be kissed, caressed, and to have physical intimacy.

There's an old story about a little boy who crawled into his parent's bed during the night. They took him back to his own room only to have him come to their bed again saying he didn't want to be alone.

"Don't you know that God is always with you?" the mom asked.

"Yes," the little boy whimpered. "But tonight I need someone with some skin!"

Sometimes I wanted someone with skin. To rest in someone's arms. To lie side-by-side. To spoon and cuddle. To make love. My husband was alive in my mind but not in the flesh. I missed his skin, his smell, his kisses, and his touch.

Physical touch is very important to the human body and psyche. According to a recent article on Health.com, ". . . touch is shaping up to be the ultimate mind-body medicine." Benefits include lowering blood pressure, heart rate, and stress hormones, increasing immune function, and relieving pain. It also releases oxytocin, the feel-good chemical in the brain.

Fortunately, I have family and friends who are huggers so I did get some physical touch. After losing Phil it seemed that we were even more touchy-feely, always hugging hello and goodbye. I also got massages.

I love a line from the hit show *Frasier* ("Look Before You Leap," Season 3 Episode 16). When Frasier's brother Niles said that he wanted to visit his ex-wife just for sex, Frasier warned him not to.

Expressing how desperate he'd been since separating from his wife, Niles confessed to Frasier that he'd been paying women to touch him.

Frasier recoiled in horror.

Niles clarified that he'd been paying for manicures, pedicures, facials and massages exclaiming, "Whenever you see a man who's well-groomed, you can bet he's not gettin' any!"

I became very well-groomed.

The Perfect First Date

About two years after Phil passed I had my first date. At least I thought it was a date.

I went to a wine tasting dinner alone and only knew one woman there. She invited me to sit with her and the guy I assumed was her date. He was nice looking, personable, and they had a friendly relationship with lots of playful banter. They'd obviously known each other for a long time. During dinner she told me that he was just a good friend and they did lots of things together. Her actual boyfriend lives out of state.

Weeks later I ran into her again and asked how her man-friend that wasn't a boyfriend was doing. The next day I got a text from him asking if I'd like to meet for a glass of wine.

We met at a nice restaurant about halfway between my place and his part of town. I was sitting at the bar and had just ordered a glass of wine when he came in. He was smart, fun, and easy to talk to. We sat there chatting and laughing for about an hour and then he asked if I had plans or if I'd like to have dinner. I chose dinner. I didn't care about the food but I wanted more conversation. It was amazing to have attention from someone who looked into my eyes, laughed at my jokes, and appeared to find me fascinating.

We discussed his work, my work, his being divorced, my being widowed, motorcycle riding, arts, and travel. The conversation easily flowed from one subject to another and we had a great deal in common.

"Have you dated much since your husband died?" he asked as dessert arrived.

"Well, that depends. Is this a date?" I joked, assuming that it was.

"No," he answered, waving his hand as if dismissing the question. "No pressure here. This is just two friends having dinner."

"In that case," I laughed, "I haven't dated at all!"

When the check came I offered to split it. After all it wasn't a date. He protested saying he'd get it this time and I could treat next time. We walked out and he waited with me for the valet to bring my car. As we said "Good night" he leaned in for a hug and kiss. I turned my cheek and gave him a warm hug. Hey, if it wasn't even a date a cheek kiss was all he was getting!

It was the perfect first date. But how could that be when he said it wasn't a date? I went out for drinks and dinner with a guy I'd recently met and he paid. I had a delightful time. With his saying it was "not a date" I didn't have to stress over whether or not he'd call again. I assumed he wouldn't. If he did it would be a while, not right away like someone who was really interested in dating me. With his saying I could treat next time, I assumed that if I wanted to invite him to accompany me to an event or to meet for dinner that he'd be open to that. No stress. No pressure. Exactly what I needed.

So what happened? A few months later I invited him to go with me to a charity event. He seemed genuinely happy that I called and we had a great time. I introduced him to another female friend that I thought he'd enjoy meeting. The three of us went to dinner a couple times. As I got to know him better I could easily see that we were not compatible as a couple. The memory remains as a perfect first date. Getting over that "first" made me feel confident that I could date.

A few friends have introduced me to men and I've met a few at social and business events. I've had a few dates in the years since but haven't fallen in love. And then there's the online dating world.

Looking for Love Online

Lots of folks are afraid of online dating. It does seem like a strange thing to shop for dates online but I guess it's no worse than the old days when people met in bars. I was single for a long time before marrying at the age of thirty-four so Phil wasn't the first guy I dated. I'm very outgoing and independent so I wasn't as afraid of going online as some women are. Plus, I know several couples who met that way and are now happily married. At this stage of life it isn't like I meet many men in my work or social life. So much other communication and connecting is online that it does make sense. I enjoy using social media so I wasn't afraid to jump in.

I was familiar with the most popular sites since I'd helped a couple single girlfriends choose photos and write profiles while I was married. First I tried Plenty of Fish because it's free and I could test the waters without financial investment. It's very popular and claims to be the world's largest online dating site. It was easy to set up a profile and easy to navigate.

It wasn't long before I emailed with several men and one asked me out. Then I froze. I told him that I realized I wasn't ready to date so soon after losing my husband. I deleted my profile and stopped shopping for men online. For a while at least.

Later I signed up for Match.com and another time for eHarmony. These are the two most popular paid sites. If you're thinking of trying online dating I recommend that you check out a few sites. Most will let you set up a profile and search for free. Then you have to subscribe before being able to contact anyone or have your profile available for people to contact you.

Beware of Catfish

Not the pond kind of catfish. The pond-scum kind.

It's important for widows and widowers to be careful because there are scammers out there. They're called "catfish" and it's their business to prey on lonely men and women who are emotionally vulnerable. They're after your money and they don't care if it's your retirement or you have to mortgage the house. Don't send money to anyone you haven't met in person and checked out.

Sending money to someone you've never met in person sounds crazy to me but it apparently happens a lot according to the *Dr. Phil* show. He's interviewed many men and women who have sent thousands of dollars, cars, and furniture to someone thinking they're in love and will soon be together with this person they've never laid eyes on. Given the lack of reality in reality TV and the need for talk shows to draw viewers with sensationalism, I'd be suspicious of the people on these shows except that my own online experience tells me they're out there. Did I mention to NEVER send money?

No, I never fell in love with a catfish and I would not send money to someone professing their love when we'd never met in person, but I did see signs of catfish. Having read about these scammers and watched too many *Dr. Phil* shows, I noticed the signs early.

Usually a catfish claims to be a widow or widower. Sad that they're giving us a bad name but it's their shtick. They usually have a young child, which in my age range is cause for a raised eyebrow. They usually have only one photo and the profile is vague with general statements and few details. They want to move off the dating site quickly to an instant message site where they're less likely to be caught and start trying to make an emotional connection right away.

Once a nice looking guy, who looked younger than his listed age (another catfish clue), emailed me. His only photo was of him on a boat. When I asked about the boat he said it belonged to a friend and he offered no other details. Anyone I know who loves boats enough to use it as a main photo would have rambled endlessly. Then he said he'd been betrayed by his last girlfriend (tugging on the heart strings) and asked if I'd ever been hurt (looking for emotional connection). I answered that people don't get to this age in life without having been hurt sometime. He asked how I'd been hurt. Assuming he'd read my profile, I replied, "Well, the whole dead husband thing was pretty painful!"

He went right into his next question without any acknowledgement of what I'd just said. He said he had a son and didn't trust anyone to keep him since the girlfriend was gone. I asked who kept the son while he was working. He said that he took the son to work with him. What? His job, which included travel, was listed as "construction" and the "son" was 10 years old, so he'd need to be in school. No man who travels internationally with a construction job is going to be dragging a ten-year-old son along with him. If your email conversation doesn't fit with the photo and the description they've posted, something's fishy. Catfishy.

My Exotic Asian Looks

Someone once emailed me with an overly flattering paragraph in broken English (another clue), saying he was so taken by my beauty and wanted to get to know me. Then he mentioned my exotic Asian looks. Huh? I'm a fair-skinned, hazel-eyed redhead. Obviously a cut and paste email. Or maybe he meant charming Irish looks.

Other Bad Guys

I had exchanged a couple emails with a local doctor. He moved to "let's meet" quickly and we planned to meet for drinks at a local sports bar. I'd omitted the search before saying "Yes," but then thought better of it. His first name wasn't common so I searched for "physician" (use the + sign) and the local part of town where he'd said he lived. Turns out he was about ten years older in his MUG SHOT! Yes, he had been arrested for phone harassment and stalking. I quickly became unavailable.

One of my friends says she doesn't add anyone she goes out with to her phone directory until she thinks they'll be around awhile. I add them as soon as I have their number. That way I can screen or block the calls if they become annoying. So far, Dr. Stalker is the only time I've needed that.

Safety First

After I've exchanged a few emails with someone, talked on the phone once or twice, and decided to meet, there are a few things I do to stay safe. I don't tell them where I live so they do not pick me up. Never for a first date. I once met a guy at a restaurant a block from my home. I drove there so he wouldn't know how close I lived. I give a general area, not the building or street when they ask where I live. I agree to meet in a public place for coffee or drinks. Never for lunch or dinner or any activity because if it turns out they're creepy or dumber than a box of rocks, I don't want to be obligated for more than a short amount of time. You can always say you have plans after. Even if your plan is to go home and watch *Scandal* on TV, that's a plan. If you're both having fun, you may be open to staying longer. If not, your getaway is already planned.

I also tell a friend who I'm meeting and where. I print out their profile, write their first and last name and phone number on it and leave it on my table. That way if I come up missing the police will have clues to start with. Maybe I've watched too many episodes of *Law and Order* but better safe than sorry, right?

Is It Worth It?

Sound like too much of a job? It can be. It can also be fun. You meet people you wouldn't otherwise cross paths with. Some you may date for a while. Some may become friends. Some may become funny dating stories to entertain your married friends with. Maybe, if you're lucky, you'll find love. I know many couples who met online and are now happily married.

So far I've met a few nice guys and collected a lot of dating stories. I've been surprised that things I thought would make me more attractive appear to make me less desirable.

I thought that not having children would make it easier since we'd have to work around the schedules of fewer people. Two men have told me that they never date women without children because they're selfish. Right. But leaving your wife and kids in a lurch so you can have a new sports car and a trophy wife half your age isn't selfish at all, is it, Mr. Divorced Stud.

When you're widowed they know there won't be a crazy ex stalking them and causing trouble, right? Some ask questions about whether we had a good marriage then they disappear. One said that he figures a divorcee will be over their ex but someone who is widowed is still in love with her dead husband. Yet I've met divorced men who are still in love with the woman who left them. Every case is different.

Many men mention thinking women are only after money and want someone who will take them places and buy them things. I'm too old for that game, have a career, and live a good life, so they shouldn't worry, right?

On a second date with a professional man who was also widowed, we were sitting in a nice restaurant having dinner and discussing travel and new restaurants around town. I thought the conversation was going well when he leaned back, folded his arms, and said, "Well, if my wife and I hadn't had children I guess we could have traveled everywhere and been to all the good restaurants!"

I was a little taken aback but didn't respond to the comment. After the check was paid, we walked out together and when the valet pulled my Mercedes to the curb he made a comment about my flashy car. Knowing that he drives a Lexus I made the comparison. "I got a good deal on my Lexus!" he fired back in defense.

"I got a good deal on my Mercedes, too," I said. It's not a new Mercedes and it isn't the very expensive sporty one that costs as much as a house so I didn't understand his objection. Later I remembered the other comment and realized that he was intimidated by his impression of my financial situation. He didn't even take time to learn that many of our exotic trips were sales incentive trips that my husband won through his work or that taking clients and their wives out to nice restaurants was part of his job. He judged me on what he guessed my life was like. He appeared to be a successful owner of a small business and lived in an affluent part of town. He'd also traveled and been to lots of nice restaurants. I was baffled by his comments.

Five Fives for Fifty-five

The year I turned fifty-five I decided to do five fives for fifty-five. That year I challenged myself to take five classes, meet five new people, have five weekend getaways, go to five new restaurants, and have five dates. Wouldn't you know the five dates was the most challenging? I'm in a city where women reportedly outnumber men eight to one and the older you are the bigger the spread. Getting a date is tough.

The first guy was a plump, polite, passive guy. I decided we could just be friends. The next guy was a widowed business man. He decided we'd just be friends. The next one was a young accountant who still lived with his mother. He was like a blond version of Sheldon on *The Big Bang Theory*. We're not friends. Next was a blind date with a widower. He asked me for a second date then cancelled by text saying that he was too distraught over his late wife. One month later he announced his engagement on Facebook.

In the fall I was wondering if I could dig up a fifth date before year end. A male friend called and asked me to have dinner with him. He is single. He asked. He paid. I claimed it as my fifth date.

Am I Relationship-Ready?

One day I was walking and thinking about my most recent date and my lack of relationships. It hit me that getting a funny story to tell my friends was almost more fun for me than having a date that I thought had real relationship possibility. I had to do some soul searching to ask myself whether I was really emotionally ready for a relationship.

Relationships have to unfold and I remember all the "will he call again" anxiety in my younger days of dating. I see my friends in "new relationship happiness" then listen to them lament when it doesn't work out or see them struggling with the push-pull of trying to figure out how to make it work for them both. Am I ready for that?

There's a good book called *Calling in The One: 7 Weeks to Attract the Love of Your Life* by Katherine Woodward Thomas, a licensed marriage and family therapist. I bought it after having lunch with two single friends who recommended it. It's a workbook style format with exercises for each chapter. Her lessons and self-help techniques help you to identify the type of relationship you want and make a list of qualities you desire in a mate along with other exercises that help you to be more available and open to relationships and to let go of beliefs that may be keeping you stuck.

These two friends, along with another woman that I know, approached the workbook as a seven-week course, doing all the exercises, reflection, and journaling. All three are now happily married. I started reading the book and doing the exercises two or three times. Each time I quit after a few chapters. Maybe I'm still not ready to be in a serious relationship. Or maybe I just haven't met the right person. Or maybe being single now is right for me. I don't know that there is one answer. Maybe one day I'll get the book out again and delve into my fears and beliefs about finding love a second time around. Or maybe not.

For now I'm happy, I have a full social calendar, and an occasional date. I'm very independent and don't mind going places alone, with girlfriends, or with couples. I have a few male friends I can call when I want to have a man attend an event with me. "Faux dates" I call them.

I don't feel a need to marry again but I'm open to the possibility that I could fall in love and change my mind.

• • •

CHAPTER 15

The Best Worst Life

"You have the best worst life," my friend June said contemplatively. After having lunch at my business club then driving home with the top down in my red convertible, we were sitting in my high-rise condo overlooking the city. "I know the worst happened," she continued, "but, Myra, you have an amazing life."

She was right. Selling "our" home and moving into "my" condo was a fresh start for me.

After moving to my condo, my friend Gayle came to visit. We've been friends for over twenty years and were besties when we were in our twenties, before either of us ever married. When she walked in tears came into her eyes. "Myra," she said, "This is what you've always wanted!" She remembered all the years ago when we'd discussed our hopes and dreams before meeting and falling in love. I grew up in the country and loved the city. She grew up in the metro area and loved the country. I married Phil and we lived in the suburbs and entertained and traveled. Our life was better than I'd ever dared imagine. She married Roger, the man of her dreams, and they live in the country with several acres of land, three dogs, and four cats. Even knowing that I'd rather have continued life with Phil, when she walked into my new home she recognized that it fit me perfectly.

I struggled a little settling into my new life. During the first year after moving to my condo I took a fiction writing class. One of the other participants was writing a book based on a young woman from the Middle East who moved to the United States to build a new life after losing her entire family in a horrific murder. The teacher pointed out that in a situation like that there is conflict between loving the life you lost and loving the new life you're creating. Conflict.

That hit me like a splash of cold water. She articulated exactly what I was feeling. I loved my life with Phil and now I was trying to build a new life. Did loving one mean I loved the other less? It seemed that the more into my new life I got the farther removed I was from my old life. It took me a while to come to terms with that conflict and feel at peace with loving my new life and letting go of the old. To accept that it wasn't just okay but it was important that I allowed myself to be happy. To embrace joy.

You Will Find Joy Again!

When I'd been widowed about a year, I thought I was doing pretty well. I was dressed, upright, and out pretending to be a business woman again. Networking has always been something I enjoy and, although I hadn't really been working with clients much since the months before Phil died, I was excited to be going to a networking event where I could reconnect with old friends and business associates.

The speaker at this event was Kathy Betty who, at the time, was owner of Atlanta's WNBA team, The Atlanta Dream. I love hearing the stories of successful women and I knew from articles in the paper that she was a widow too. Her husband Gary Betty, CEO of EarthLink, had died of cancer a couple years before Phil died. After hearing her speak about the importance of sports to girls and young women I went up to shake her hand and tell her I'd enjoyed her talk. I mentioned that I, too, was recently widowed.

She took my hand in both of hers and drew her face close to mine. "Look into my eyes. Do you see the joy there? You will find joy again," she said firmly. "I know it may not seem like it now, but you will."

My eyes filled with tears. I'll never forget her words. "You will find joy again." On days when I was struggling I remembered her words and clung to them for hope.

Creating a Life I Love

There's a line in the movie *Shawshank Redemption* where Andy Dufresne, who's serving time for a murder he didn't commit, says that it comes down to a choice to "get busy living or get busy dying."

Before I sold our old house, I decided it was time to get busy living and I gave a lot of thought to where I wanted to be and how I wanted my day-to-day life to look. "Our" house was too big and too expensive for me to stay in. I knew I wanted to stay in the Atlanta area. I wanted to live in a high-rise in a walkable area. I wanted a community feel and to be in a convenient area. Now I have all that.

I have a sense of community although I live in a busy in-town area. I've gotten to know several neighbors and often run into them when I walk to the grocery store where we all know the cashier by name. Recently on my morning walk I ran into a waiter at a local restaurant that I frequent and we stopped to chat. Several times at the post office I've seen people I know from business networking groups. I see someone I know at a nearby mall much more frequently than I did when I lived in the suburbs.

I've held on to old friends and made new ones. It's easy to find friends to go to the movies with or to meet someone for a glass of wine. When I lived in the suburbs I had a couple friends in the neighborhood but they were usually busy with their children. My nearest close friend was about five miles away and most others were at least ten miles away. Now I have several single women friends in the same building with me and probably ten others within walking distance. There's always something to do around here. A homeowner's social, the opening of a new restaurant, a book signing at a nearby store, a charity fundraising event, or wine tasting. I love all the convenient options for entertainment and the proximity of people to share them with.

I made it a point to consciously build into my life people I loved being around and things I loved doing. Phil dying at such an early age under-scored for me the importance of enjoying life on a daily basis. It was also important to me that I have work I enjoy. When I was ready to rebuild my speaking and writing business I thought about what I really enjoy doing and who I enjoy working with.

Enjoy Life and Do Good

I have always been philosophical, looking for meaning and purpose in life and its events. I study life. Phil lived life. He didn't try to analyze it. That was one of the attributes I loved most about him. Maybe that's why I'm the one left behind—to analyze, to reflect upon the deeper learning.

About a month before Phil died he was in neuro-ICU after severe seizures. I was sleepless one night, praying that God wouldn't take him from me so soon. Looking for guidance and comfort I reached for my Bible. It fell open to Ecclesiastes Chapter 3. The passage starts, "To every-thing there is a season, and a time to every purpose under the heaven . . ." I've read and heard this many times before, as I'm sure you have. Back in 1965 The Byrds used the words in the lyrics of a song called "Turn! Turn! Turn!" It's remained popular for decades.

This time I read beyond the familiar verses. The author, who according to Biblical scholars was reflecting on the meaning of life, goes on to explain that whatever man's works may be, there is no way that we can understand God's plan from beginning to end. He says, "I know there is no good in them but for a man to rejoice and do good in his life. And that every man should eat and drink and enjoy the good of all his labour, it is the gift of God." As I read and re-read this Bible passage I realized that although Phil never professed or defined a life philosophy, I think this verse sums it up— "rejoice and do good."

That's the way he lived. He lived life rejoicing. Whether people knew him well or only met him briefly they often commented on his bright eyes, big smile, and happy nature. He also "did good" in both small and big ways. He did well in his work, in his accomplishments and in his adventures. He enjoyed "the good of all his labor." Phil was generous and kind, of-ten helping others with no expectation for return. "Rejoice and do good." That's the way Phil lived.

After Phil's diagnosis I found where he had written in his journal a quote from the Farmer's Almanac: "A long life may not be good enough but a good life is always long enough." Beneath it Phil wrote, "I've had a good life!"

Rejoice and do good is what my amazing husband taught me. I modernized the wording into "Enjoy life and do good" and adopted that as the new tagline for my business. Beyond a tag line, it is my mantra for how I aim to live each day. The writer Joseph Addison said, "Three grand essentials to happiness in this life are something to do, something to love, and something to hope for." My purpose is to use my speaking and writing to help others to enjoy life and do good. My new normal is to work with purpose, live with passion and make a difference. So although I lost the love of my life, I have built a life that I love. Kathy Betty was right. I have found joy again. I hope and pray that you will too!

• • •

If the only prayer you ever
say in your entire life is
thank you, it will be enough.

Meister Eckhart

Acknowledgments

This book would not have been possible without the ideas, encouragement, critiques and gentle shoves from friends and advisors Sam Horn, Vikki Locke, Nanette Littlestone, June Cline, Susan Reece, and Vanessa Lowry. Thank you for all your support.

Dr. Robin Kirby, thank you for your wisdom and guidance as I struggled through the most difficult time of my life. My former mastermind group, Sally Jamara, Lissa Versteegh, Tamara O'Neil, and Elisha Bailez, thank you for listening and for referring me to Robin.

My family—Elaine White, Cynthia Williamson, Christopher Williamson, Dot Zimmerlee, Max, Donna and Ken McElhaney, Kevin and Kenneth Bills, and all my nieces and nephews—thank you for loving me even when I was thoughtless or seemed a bit crazy.

To our fabulous friends who surrounded us while Phil was sick and took care of me after he was gone—Jennifer Bristol, Ted Gaillard, Larry and Susan Garrard, Roger and Gayle Gilbreth, Robin Hensley, Ron Carpenter and Rhonda Hausman, Mike Hughes, Mark Johnson, Steve Rawlston, Brenda Reese, Jean Shore, Melany and Terry Ward, Elaine Weatherby, Mark Whittmyer, and Gary Williamson.

All the folks at Occam Networks. Thank you for being so supportive to Phil during his illness and to me after he passed. He loved working with y'all.

They say that *"a friend is someone who knows the song in your heart and can sing it back to you when you've forgotten the words."* Thank you to my dear friends (old and new) who helped me remember who I was and find myself again as I moved forward—Kathy Betty, Connie Bowers, Cynthia

Camilleri, Nancy Chambers, Bonnie Daneker, Josh Elrod, Essie Escobedo, Sandy Hoffman, Bobbi Kornblit, Jennifer Langley, Tricia Molloy, Ronda Rich and all my great neighbors at The Oaks. A special thank you to a couple of dear friends who passed away last year. Marilynn Mobley was always there with advice and encouragement. Mary Ann Carbonell, whom I met a few years after Phil passed, showed me how to have fun again.

Thank you to you, my readers. Meeting so many widowed people in the last few years gave purpose to my writing. I hope you find encouragement through my story. I wish you renewed joy and I pray that you're surrounded with love and comfort as you move forward in building a life you love after your loss.

• • •

About the Author

With over 20 years' experience in speaking and writing, Myra McElhaney has worked with clients such as Coca-Cola, AT&T and Delta Technology. She traveled the US speaking to audiences across a broad spectrum of industries including banking, telecommunications, transportation and many more.

Myra speaks for companies, associations and conferences and is often asked to do keynote or breakout sessions on topics related to women in the workplace. Having interviewed over 100 accomplished women and served on the boards of various women's organizations, she has a breadth of knowledge about issues specific to women.

Myra is author of *Mama Always Says. . .* and *Musings on Major and Minor Matters that May or May not Matter.* She's co-author of *The Sun Sisters Guide to the Girlfriends Perfect Beach Vacation* and *CLIMB: Leading Women in Technology Share Their Journeys to Success.* Her interview on Happiness Recipe Radio was included in the book, *Happiness Recipe: Whippin' up happiness with wit, wisdom and wonderful food!*

Myra's writing has appeared in magazines and newspapers including *Little Pink Book, Atlanta Women's Magazine,* and *Gwinnett Business Journal.* Her advice is often quoted in publications such as *Investor's Business Daily, McCall's, Woman's World, PowerSelling,* and the *Atlanta Journal and Constitution.*

Visit Myra's website and follow her on social media for news about upcoming projects or to contact her to speak for your group.

www.MyraMcElhaney.com

Thank you for reading
Building a Life You Love AFTER Losing the Love of Your Life.

I hope you found encouragement through my story. I wish you renewed joy and I pray that you're surrounded with love and comfort as you move forward in building a life you love after your loss.

www.MyraMcElhaney.com